Reflections

01/28/2015

Dear Kareem,

Let me start off by saying I know it's been a long time since the two of us exchanged any words. Therefore, if you find this letter not saying much, I hope you understand that after all these years I don't know what to converse with you about.

It kinds of feels like you're a complete stranger. Although knowing how you're doing is still something that crosses my mind.

I know you don't know how much the role you played in my life for that period of time has impacted me. All I really been trying to tell you over the years was, Thank You, for help shaping me into the woman I've become.

I would love to have the chance to just sit down and kick it with you. Let me know if your up for the visit and I'll come through.

Shanequa

Freeze,

Wassup Big Cuz? Sitting on the runway waiting to take off! It's none other than, "young esquire, ain't none flyer". If someone asks, just call me "cash"! I'm so fly I leave my footprints in the sky!

Nah, Wassup cuz, this is Cash, hope by the time you receive this letter you're in good spirits. You know, "trap my body but not my mind". "Just a minor setback, still in all we living just think about the "Get Back". For starters, I miss you, love you as well. I'm from Far Rock, I had no Rich, Alpo's, A.Z., no Preme, or Boy George. You know what I'm saying but I had **YOU** for all that is worth! I learn a lot about this life of ours from you. Class, Respect, Humbleness, Enjoyment, Patience as well as reaction. What I mean by reaction is: I got this thing I go by two approaches. You could take one approach which is what I call the Gandhi effect or approach and two the Hitler effect or approach. I tend to take the Gandhi approach which most will take as a weakness but they don't understand the wisdom, the brains and respect behind it. The reaction brings longevity and more production to your being and business as well as your environment and you get what you need. Other than that, I'm cooling, can't complain, just waiting my turn. Truth be told I will be me but it will not be the same without you there and Looch but I'm sailing. Just rolling with the wind and waves. Where I am at now, just remaining at peace. Ain't nothing like it, Word! I'm on a mission. Been through too much. I'm pushing to surround myself amongst different caliber of people. I always wish and want the best for others. Nah, mainly us, word! I look thru the rearview mirror and see where we came from. Then wipe my forehead and say "shit, we still here when we shouldn't be, according to most" Standing firm with my head to the creator like, "yo, what up, we still here, why?" But with all thanks and acknowledgements for the air we still inhale. Two things about me many may not know. One, I never been in-love with no woman and I fear nothing but poverty. All my love and loyalty lies with yall, my family and those that stand with us. At times I wonder about you? How you feeling? What's on your mind? Just like me,

3

you are a Pisces and I know I distance myself just to see others thru their situation. So I ask you, what's on your mind? What's your thoughts?

"Every man is the Architect of his own Fortune"

I wrote that because it reminds me of **you**. Just thought I share that with you. If you ever wonder the effect you have on people, you have a great one on me. Whatever you face and deal with, just be yourself and remember what you built. Not just far as capitol but the love, loyalty and bonds you built with me and many others. You know for ME that shits unbreakable, as they say now FACTS BRO!

CASH

Kareem,

I must say that this was by far one of the most touching letters I've ever received. I know tons of people and they swear that they know me so well.... False! I can honestly say that you do. I have yet to meet a person that can fill your shoes for the role you play in every ones life. I mean that. Not just how people view you, but Im speaking about in life. I say that with all sincerity. NO one has given me as much insight on things as you have, or criticized me in a good way without making me feel unsure of myself or without it benefiting solely them. Youve never put me in a harmful situation or ever asked me to compromise my feelings or saftey for your own gain. Im not saying that everybody does, but it does happen. Youve said to me before "You cant love everyone the same". You are right. Sometimes its hard for me to not be all in because Im caring and supporting. At times I sit and think about my many "situations".... how they came about and how they ended. Sometimes I wish I couldve been less supportive (LOL). It wouldve probably saved me 1,000 headaches.

I really hope everything that you want and dream of comes true. No because I fit in there somewhere, but because you

5

really deserve it. You have always been the
go to person ... The "Mr Fix It" The "Mr
Get Rid of this Problem" even if it doesnt
involve you in any way. I highly doubt
that there are many that you could go
to and get the same in return. When the
chips are down, its Kareem to the rescue.
You have one of the biggest hearts. Don't
get me wrong you are mean as hell when
you want to be, but I've learned to understand
your meaness to me (Lol) Alot of people
feel like I get away with the most
when it comes to you, and sometimes
I know I do! I know that I have a soft
spot in your heart. (You have created a
spoiled brat). I admire your drive, your
consistency, your ability to know what
youre going to accomplish by all means
necessary. That takes alot of dedication
and discipline because sometimes it so
easy to get distracted. I know for me it
is. I dislike that about myself, because
I know that there are alot of things that
I should've accomplished. If I've learned
nothing else, I've learned that anything you
want, you have to work hard for.... NO
matter how easy the next man makes it
look.

That compliment that you gave me and
the way you described me ..... really
means alot to me.. I thank you so much

→

6

You know me so well. You've helped me grow into the strong woman that I am. You told me "Fuck letting other people down, never let yourself down"... Those words are gonna stay with me for ever and a day. I will forever cherish our friendship. People don't get genuine friendships like this often.... Until next time

Tamara

I want to give this shout out to my brother "Ice", in the completion of your book. "Congratulations". You know I can think of a few other nicknames that will fit besides "Ice", inspire, determine, focus, prosper, so it's no surprise to me that you completed this project.

Ice let me touch on your book; it took me on a fast pace lifestyle of drugs, money and the end result of that lifestyle, jail and death... but what's diffrent about your book is that it sends the message that there are options even for us.

Ice after all our laps around the yard and the talks we had, and the many times we sat down and played 5000 and talked; I realize what makes you tick... you're driven to be the best at what you do.

You'll go that extra mile to get the job done. That's a quality I have to say I admire about you.

I read this recently in a book and it stuck with me for some reason, it went like this...

Opportunities are useful only to those who were prepared to seize them.

Gifts were appreciated only by those whose minds were equipped to see their value.

I want you to know Ice, I seize the opportunity, and I appreciate you becoming my friend.

Your brother in the struggle
Quest

I'll be coming around the mountain, when I come   →

8

Acknowledgement

This dream of mine to get this book which are my views on the world in which I live in would not be possible without the help of two important and dedicated people. Skip and Kim rode this process of writing and editing my terrible handwriting. They stayed patient with me when I became anxious to get the book to print. They never complained about using up their time to help me when they both have families of their own. I cannot thank Kim and Skip enough. Not to many people that lived on the edge as I did could have such positive and giving people to step forward and understand what I was trying to do. Kim being an accomplished editor was such a plus for me to have in my corner. A New York Times bestselling editor. Both Skip and Kim are from my projects in Ravenswood Houses. College educated with great careers. I wonder at times how I can be connected to people from both sides of the road and both sides willing to help me with my ventures. Life's journey cannot be predicted for anyone. I certainly couldn't predict writing a book. I want to thank everyone who supported my vision in writing my book. I hope my truth inspires more people to reach inside themselves and pull their passions to the forefront and shoot for the stars. I look at Kim and Skip as my angels that guided me to stay on the path of finishing this chapter of my life. If they would have been too busy I probably would have put the idea of writing my book to the back of mind to collect dust like so many other lost dreams.

Special thanks to all the inmates (people) who read the manuscript and told me it must be published

- Ben Johnson (Pitt) Africa
- Alonzo Powell (Zo) Elmira
- Keston Braithwaite-(Kae) BK
- "B: Harris-BK
- Robert Tartt-Savannah Ga
- Jacob- Buffalo
- Eric Harris (Quest)-Syracuse
- Jay Mills –Harlem
- Pistol- Bx
- Hov-Eastside Harlem
- Quiet- Buffalo
- Maurice Eady-Poughkeepsie
- L.S.-Syracuse
- Maurice Knight-Long Island
- Major-Buffalo
- Gambino-Queens

This book is based on a journey that had many good times and many bad times. This is a story that many minorities live through which isn't spoken about. This is one man's truth and his views on society and politics and oppression. The names and events have been altered for privacy reasons. This is a story of pain, love, loyalty, betrayal and evolution. The story is blunt and speaks hard reality. In a perfect world the reader will get the right message, but we don't live in a perfect world. As you read keep your mind open and try to look at life through the eyes of the people that are poor and struggling to have a better life. That "American Dream" that the government tells you to chase after. You cannot be raised in a capitalist country and expect people not to chase the almighty dollar by the means they know. I was told that I would get criticized for not taking a definitive stance on certain issues in this book. I fought myself about that while I was writing, and came to the conclusion that my conscience would not let me delete any truths from my beliefs. Therefore, I know that some parts of society will not agree with parts of this book. If you haven't walked down my path then you wouldn't understand my stance. Let's work on solutions and not judge too much.

People say that experience is the best teacher I am one that doesn't believe that is true. I am a firm believer that you can learn from the mistakes of others. In this book I give some graphic accounts of some of the experiences I have had so that you can get a full emotional effect of how dangerous the life I led was. I want to show that the street life can be much worse than society chooses to recognize and believe. Though there are good times shared here, you must realize the COST of those good times. The price for me was my freedom and on several occasions, nearly my life. Through the decades I have become immune to crime and indifferent to it as well. The streets made me a hardened man. This is no life to lead to have a few dollars. It took most of my life to start thinking about changing my route to riches. I still want riches but I'm ready to get it on society's terms to an extent. I want men and women, young and old, that have no direction and are at a crossroads in their lives to read this book, acknowledge my choices and the consequences of those choices, and make better decisions for themselves. In the 90's the NYC murder rate was 2,000-2,200 annually, now it is less than 500. I was a teenager in those days and caught in the street life. I became a product of my environment. This book was written to scare you so that you don't become the product of a similar environment you may find yourself in today. Learn from my experiences, not your own.

Part I

From the Womb

to

Prison Tombs

So where do I begin? Do I start by telling you where I am writing this from, or do I wait until the end to let you know what you probably know? Yes, I am in prison. I'm on Rikers Island waiting to go upstate for a couple of years. I am not crying or disappointed because I came to know that sooner or later this would happen! I am just glad that I didn't get my lights put out like so many of the great hustlers before me. Like Jay-Z said, "Everyone has their story." At some point in my story, you might know someone like me or at other times you probably won't. It all depends on the way you were raised, what kind of values your family had or how observant you were as a child. It also might depend on how far you were willing to go to get what you wanted for yourself. As well as what you wanted and needed for your family. Well here is my story...

This is a true story about me. I'm not trying to bash anyone along the way. Their story is their own, their view is not mine. I feel I always thought a little different from my friends. Maybe I just used a deeper thought process. It's like when two people look at a painting and they both interpret it differently. Same painting, different outlooks. This is how the world was to me. I had so many positive people involved in my life. I learned from my parents, coaches, teachers, friends and even lessons from books. Therefore, I cannot make an excuse for the path I chose to follow. I also had the dark side of the world around me. The crazy thing is that the negative influences were from people who were also parents, coaches, teachers, friends, and my friend's parents. How weird is that? I feel that you have to find the balance in everything and sort out what's right and make the right decision. Well, after all is said and done, let's get my story started because it might take a while.

Let me begin back in 1973, when I was born on March 19th on my sisters second birthday. I guess I ruined that day for her! As far back as I can remember I watched everything people did around me and stayed out of grown folks' business. I was never the one to want to be in the spotlight around adults, but with my friends, I never stayed in the background. I grew up in the Ravenswood Housing Projects in Long Island City, Queens. This was a place where people from some other neighborhoods might consider us middle class, maybe even rich. It was neither; it's just that the housing projects all around us were way poorer. On one side, Ravenswood was four blocks away from Queensbridge Houses Projects. Yes, Queensbridge: the largest public housing project in

America made up of a labyrinth of 96 buildings. The majority of families had a host of brothers and sisters. You don't meet too many people from "Q.B." that are from a single child household. On the other side of Ravenswood was a small project called Astoria Housing Projects. Astoria Projects was much smaller than Q.B. and Ravenswood and primarily a poor, black neighborhood. Ravenswood is made up of 45 buildings over four blocks.

We had every nationality living there; Whites, Blacks, Spanish, Russians, Chinese etc. It was a real melting pot and the beginning of the American dream. People used their time in my neighborhood to better themselves and eventually move out of the projects to buy homes. This is what the projects were actually made for. So, I have seen many things early that were positive in life that my friends from the other two neighborhoods didn't see. Kids from Ravenswood and Queensbridge went to school together from Kindergarten until you left Junior High School, if you went to the local schools, or until you finished high school if you chose the local options. Most of my friends down my way went to the parochial schools like St. Rita's, St. Patrick's or Queens Lutheran School. However I didn't, I went right down the block to P.S. 112 for first and second grade, and then P.S. 111 for grades three through six. My junior high school, J.H.S. 204, was a wild ass school. In my projects back then, parents were strict and we all had curfews. When we came outside, we played sports like football, soccer, wrestling, boxing, baseball, and punch ball; anything that the park in front of my building could handle. I played with my Spanish friends Danny, Ralph, Joey and my man Dillon, Johnny, Jimmy, Dread, Philip, Steve, and a few others. These were the guys that lived on my side of the block. From the names you can see it was a mixed crowd. They were all good guys and we had fun together as kids, spending the night over each other's houses. Danny and Dillon's families spoiled them. I loved staying over either of their houses because we watched cable TV at the time, and they had plenty of toys and games. Dillon left while we were very young so I don't remember if they even knew each other.

I also had a bunch of friends from Q.B. that I loved because we all were in Head Start together and they were more hip to different things. Like I said Q.B. was a different animal. There were always basketball tournaments, kids hanging out late, and people outside playing music. You would see drug dealers with fancy cars, chains, murders, shootings. You know, all the street life shit. It fascinated me! I was totally in awe of violence and doing things with my friends just to see if we could get away with it. This was my crew: Ocean, Los,Cliff, Ramone, Lloyd, Peace, Julius, and Joe-Shan. There were more to come, but this was the first group of soon to be "top goons." I hung out with Ocean. Ocean and I go so far back that we were known as cousins up until the nineties. We could have probably kept that lie going but we got too old for that. We were very close though. Carlos was just as close with us but nobody would have gone for that if we said we were all cousins! In reality, we were all like brothers. The three of us had known each other since we were 3 years old. Los was a jokester. He always committed pranks and bothered dudes. He did it for fun but more like fun for just him. He had a big heart, but really ranked and played way too much. His Mom was the mother you'd wish you had. She knew the street and had a lot of ties to the street. Los was spoiled by the number runners and drug dealers because they respected his mother and their family. Hood Love is the best love because you are exempt from problems other kids have. Ocean on the other hand made his mark by just being a tough kid. If he fucked with you, he fucked with you hard. He had a temper that got him into trouble but he didn't care, he was getting the same respect in life as Los but for different reasons.

Queensbridge was already like a big family, but certain dudes got more love than others and these two were on the top of that list. I loved being out there in Q.B. We played regular games like tag and hot peas and butter, and also played sports, mostly basketball. In my hood I didn't play much basketball when I was young because there was no basketball court on my block so we played a lot on their block in Queensbridge. The afterschool center and CYO programs were set up for children to join teams and to play each other in tournaments. When we were in about fourth or fifth grade, Super Ed moved to Q.B. He came to my class which was the top class in the school; I was in the smartest classes from first grade until I went to high school. I even got skipped from seventh grade to ninth grade. They teased me by calling me a nerd. It's so ignorant that we thought that being called a nerd was an insult. That's a joke that at my age, I would now gladly accept! Well Super and I clicked quickly. Ocean, Los, Cliffy and the rest of the guys didn't think that Super was tough enough to hang with us at first. But because he lived on the block, dudes gave him a chance and he became one of the best friends we ever had. We were all competitive over everything, whether we were playing video games, racing, playing basketball or fighting. We play fought and wrestled with each other a lot. We slap boxed all the time. I remember when we played on St. Rita's CYO team; the coach told us if we scored 100 points we would get a pizza party. How do you tell ghetto kids that? We played rough against the White kids that went to those Catholic schools and we knew we would kill them. One time we beat a team 120-10. I know that sounds crazy, but we took no prisoners! We beat another team 108-8, and we were eating our damn pizza. We were regular kids doing regular things. Shit, wasn't everyone doing the things we were doing? Where the fuck did things take a drastic turn in my life? How did I go from hanging with the fellas and playing sports to getting deep into the damn drug game? Reflecting I think this extreme competiveness lead me to my negative behavior, it made me think I always must succeed. It's something I think hard about. This is something I think about often.

I also spent my summers out in Far Rockaway A/K/A the sixth borough to some people. My Grandmother lived in Edgemere

Projects. Yeah, it was a real war zone area! This housing project was so wild that people in the other projects out there would refuse to go there. My Grandmother lived in 441 Beaches 51st Double building. There was never a damn dull moment out there! I loved when I came to visit my Grandmother and my friends there. Sometimes my Mom pulled in the parking lot and I wouldn't even go upstairs to my Grandmother's, but instead, I'd run to my friends and start to play. I was known for playing basketball out there. I used to do work in their tournaments. I would tell them I was from L.I.C. (Long Island City) but they would just always mess it up and say I was from Long Island. Dudes were bugged out for that. I had great friends there also that ended up being gangsters in their own right. I ran around mostly with Johnny from the second floor and Cheese that lived next door to him and my man Marvin, who had a few other brothers, Mitchell, Jo-Jo and Wonderful. Then there was Marious, Anton, and Marlon with the burnt face, Timmy, Nat, Eddie and their older brother Thomas. Again there was a lot of fighting going on in this environment. Play fighting as well as real. A lot of weed dealing from Rasta Chris crib and I believe Big Bob that had those German Shepherds, also had the weed clicking too. All of this was way before crack. Dudes sold bud (weed) and dudes in the rock used Angel Dust. So, the beginning of my life there was fights and sports.

In Edgemere they used to have building fights. This shit was pre-arranged, and at a certain time, the guys from each building crushed each other with bats, belts, bricks, sticks, and just went crazy on each other. Out there is where I first knew a young kid getting killed on purpose. He was about 13 or 14 years old but he was a wild dude. So at times it was scary to be out there but it helped mold me to be tough. So part of who I am is because of that environment. There were a lot more guys from the building that I left out because they were either younger than me or much older, but one guy I want to mention is Marlon and Jermaine's little brother Javon. Javon was always bad. I mean you'd have to whip his ass bad because he liked to spit on people and just start bullshit. He ended up being a menace to society out there as he grew up. Shooting and robbing everything that moved. They named him Joker and he was on the TV show, America's Most Wanted, before they caught up to him. Life dealt him a bad hand and he played it all the way out. I wonder if it had anything to do with what he saw as a young kid. His oldest brother robbed the cable man or some type of worker as the guy sat in his car under my Grandmother's window. His brother stuck the gun through the window and told the driver to pass something over. I'm not sure what it was. The guy tried to pull off and was shot in the head. He became a vegetable. I can't forget the day his brother was arrested. It was raining and they had him lying face down on the ground and everyone was outside watching. Although he is out of prison now, I have never seen him again. These environments with the events taken place was shaping my mind to falsely believing that this was just the way life was.

My man Johnny was a good dude. He was a little older than me and respected me on the ball courts. He had a friend named Scooter who was like his mentor that was crazy nice in ball and I hung out with them. Johnny had cousins from the other side of the projects and he would bring me back there sometimes. Over there I would have to slap box with dudes and Johnny let me know that I couldn't avoid some type of violence out there. There were plenty of goons in Edgemere to go around, from Sha-Wells and Pac-man to G-fresh, Ron Love and Rome. I also had a close friend out there named Wayne. He was a really good friend and nice in basketball and probably the only dude that I hung out with, who didn't live in the building. I remember one day I came to visit my Grandma as I got older, and I heard he caught some bodies in Ohio and was about to get the death penalty. I was in shock because I knew he wasn't a punk but didn't know he would get caught up in something that deep. From what I heard he was paid to go to Ohio with some older dudes that were getting drug money, to serve as a bodyguard. But I heard that when they got there, he and another dude killed the guys they were supposed to protect AND the guys they were buying the drugs from. I heard it went smoothly but dudes came back to New York talking about it and they got arrested. Could it be that stories like this were the reason that my mind started to lean towards crime? I wonder.

My family life was cool I guess. By today's standards, the doctors might say that it wasn't. But no matter what I saw I knew the difference between right and wrong plus my mother and father were the "Do as I say, not as I do" type of parents. I loved my parents. My Mom was very important to me. She instilled values like having to work to get money. If I didn't do my chores, then I didn't get my allowance. Plus, I might get an ass whipping. It was legal back then. It should be legal now. Without fearing your parents during the beginning stages of your growth as a child, you're likely to head down the wrong path when you live in our type of environment. I feared and respected my parents, period! My Mom never let me miss school. I used to get awards for perfect attendance. Not good or excellent but perfect! That means no days were to be missed for Christ's Sake!! These were some of the things that were important in molding my life, as well as the influence of great teachers that I had. My Assistant Principal was a Black man (Mr., Elder); my most influential teacher was a Black woman (Ms. Rice). Even my principal was a Black woman named Ms. Barry. All of my teachers liked me because I was smart, respectful and athletic. I was president of my class, the G.O. (General Organization) and of the whole elementary school. We really had an election and we had to put posters up and debate and do everything like a real election. I won in a landslide. My education and my teachers were the balance on the positive side that kept me from falling into just being bad.

My Dad was a serious alcoholic. He really got me sick. I know it's an addiction but he made life hard for us because it strained the marriage with my mother until she had to put him out.

One night he came home drunk and my mom told him to stop drinking and snatched the liquor bottle out his hand and they began to fight. He started choking her really hard and me and my sister were yelling and trying to break it up. My Mom hit him in the head with the bottle as he was choking her, but it didn't break and fell to the floor and broke. I ran and got my bat and hit the motherfucker on the head and he let her go. The police were called and he had to go. Back in those days, the husband didn't get arrested. He just had to take a walk and cool off. I guess over the years too many people were killed after that walk because I am in jail now with people who are where they are for just the threats to choke their women. This world is crazy.

Even though I am a semi-private person when it comes to my personal life, I do love both sides of my family and my in-laws. The situation with my father and I kept me from enjoying the company of family on his side. I was raised by my mother and on holidays and summers vacations as a child, I spent time with my grandmother, aunts and uncles on my maternal side. I knew all my cousins (most) from my mother's siblings. We were all kind of close. My mother had four brothers and two sisters; she was the oldest of all. My father's side on the other hand, I remember a few cousins growing up but I wasn't in contact with them, even though they lived probably a half hour away. That side of my family was much bigger than my Mom's. I believe my paternal grandmother had between 14 and 18 children. On that side I have mostly women, beautiful women at that. I have aunts and cousins that love me to death. I wish I would have had a closer relationship with them as a child. Maybe I didn't because they were girls and I was a boy. The alcoholism in me comes from my Dad's side. This side of the family are heavy drinkers. They also can get really rowdy just like me. As we became adults, we began to get back in contact with one another and became close. When I see any of them there are no awkward moments. And I can feel nothing but positive energy toward me. In the early 2000's I decided to host a BBQ for them. It turned out beautiful. They showed up with their children, boyfriends, husbands, and grandkids. They were able to meet my son for the first time as well. I supplied all the food and of course there was plenty of champagne. It was a great introduction back to a family situation between all of us. To this day I'd be overjoyed to see any of them again. I was busy running the streets and working hard so I didn't attend many family functions. The few I did though, I made sure I made an impact for my family. My sister keeps in contact more with that side of the family and even with my father. At this point I don't hate him but I don't care for him. I can see him or not, it doesn't matter to me. The rest of the family I want to be involved in their lives forever. Let's toast to the CULBERTSONs.

It's a funny thing about running into family later in life. You get a better understanding of why you are the way you are. You see similarities with your cousins, aunts and uncles. Maybe that you walk the same, have the same charm, smooth skin etc... But you see a part of yourself in them. In some instances you can figure things out about yourself by looking deep into your family members. Seeing their flaws, you might figure out yours and what other people complain about you. DNA is powerful. There are still a lot that doctors and scientists don't know about DNA. I have my mother's complexion and height. I have my father's brain and balding condition SHIT! Wish he didn't have that. My uncles and I are prone to crime and being in jail or prison along with every damn near male cousin. We are all strong willed, stubborn as well. Some of this comes from DNA, and some from economics and lack of education. Anyway these are the secrets children keep in until they cannot keep them in any longer. This was the eighties when they had the "Say No to Drugs" campaign. This was the early eighties when to me smoking weed was the worst drug someone could do. I felt that way because that's what I was taught in school. My mother smoked weed and drank, but not drink like my father. I probably had never seen her drunk but I've seen her high. That was devastating and embarrassing to me. I knew my friends from Far Rockaway and Q.B.'s parents did the same. But I didn't think that my Ravenswood friends' parents did. One night I was coming home and as I was walking down the hallway to my door, I smelled weed. I had my friends with me, and inside I was crushed. No one ever said anything but they probably did when they got home.

I think that about the seventh grade we started to get our hands on guns. Not too many but we probably had a .22, a .25 and a 380. We were not using them every day but they were on deck. I think Ocean was able to get them for us. Back then, people were selling them like crazy. We didn't carry guns everyday but we were sure to get into trouble every day. Jumping people, robbing people and things like that. You see, these are the years to get your rep up. Without your rep up anything you try to do later will be useless in the streets. So you would go around and play the knockout games, as they call them now. We didn't look for old men and women but looked for dudes our age. Yeah they didn't have to be doing shit and we would pounce and rob them. As a man in his forties, I see how foolish this shit was. Kids try that today and they end up in jail. That type of shit that was kind of like bullshit to us is now making the news. Times has changed I tell you. So you can see, the balance was tipping over to the negative side. My father was a drunk and Mom used weed, which at the time was so bad that it was my equivalent to crack. Then it became a single parent household where my mother couldn't get my sister and me everything we wanted anymore. My mother worked every day and cooked every night. My allowance disappeared but I still had to do the chores. Again, I blame no one for the rest of the decisions I made in my life.

Like I said we were all competitive and that came to the street violence and robberies etc. I remember a time when Ocean and Ramone caught some pimps on Queens Plaza where they used to be a hoe track and they ended up with a few grand. They ran through the block and told me and Super. Shit, we immediately wanted to get some money. Super went and got the guns and we went. I told him not to bring the guns because I didn't want to shoot anyone in a robbery. It's bad enough we were taking something from someone but to shoot him also, would have been overkill! Super figured 'Nah we will just scare him yada, yada, yada.' We found our mark and got up on him. Super pulled out the gun but the pimp didn't back down. Maybe he looked at us like we were little kids or whatever but he didn't give us shit. I instantly started beating this pimp motherfucker. Super pointed the pistol at him. He was fighting back but we scared the shit out of him with the gun. I didn't even remember if we got shit. If we did there weren't any stacks but we fucked that dude up.

He didn't shoot the pimp and I was glad but over the years we started getting crazy. Now we were about to end the eighties.

We all sell a little crack now. I think my man Geno and Ramone were hustling first, then Ocean. Not sure when Super started or Los but everyone was doing it. Me, I took work (crack) from the older guys in my projects and hustled in my hood. I used to get paid 70/30 split off every hundred I sold. I got the latter amount. I hustled for anyone in my neighborhood that gave me a pack. From Universal and Majestic to my man G-Man to Raymond. Raymond paid me the best giving me 35 dollars of every hundred I sold. This was new for me. I usually just sold two hundred and took the seventy bucks and hung out with my crew down in Queensbridge. We were still into sports at that time and girls. We had a crew of girls that we hung out with. Shit was like the movie Grease. A group of guys that hung with a group of girls. In about '87 or '88, a dude that impacted my life in a big way, came into the picture. His name was Big D. He was from the Bronx. I first met the guy playing basketball in the park behind his sister's building. He came to live with her because of some stuff that happened in the Bronx. He was a big Black dude that had a big heart and had a lot of personality and was funny. My man put him on our team on the court and he played, but I didn't want this nigga on our team. My man Joe said let him play. We won a few games. He then sat down and they began to talk. Big D was a young kid also. He was a few years older than me but only one year older than my man Joe. Joe and Big D talked about drugs in the projects. Who was doing what, etc? Big D said he had nickels on him of crack and he wanted to sell in our hood. It was a known fact that if you didn't live in our neighborhood you were not selling drugs out there. Big D showed Joe his bottles that he packaged in pink tops and they were like three times the size of the bottles guys had in Queens. So Joe told Big D to give him the bottles and he will sell them. Joe could break off the five dollars and make another ten off every bottle. Simple math. We all started hanging out and they were getting money. I still only took packs here and there but I was still robbing dudes and selling Polo gooses and chains and rings to the hustlers in my hood. After a while Big D and I got really tight like brothers and he eventually started pumping for himself in the hood and was making plenty of money because he cooked his shit up whereas people were still buying cook up on our side. Whatever I went through, this dude supported me. We were like brothers. He still had a crew from the Bronx that came through and hung out from time to time. I wasn't too fond of them and they were not of me either, except for his man Scott. His brother Damon and I were cool but he had a flip side to him. The rest of them felt they didn't like my relationship with Big D because he looked out for me heavily.

I was the first person to introduce him to Bloomies and Macy's and shit like that. He was a Bronx nigga that shopped on 145th at KP Kong and places like that. He was a hood shopper. Champion and chukkas. All type of Timberlands. Army jackets with the hat to match. LIC hustlers were wearing Polo, Guess, Tommy and Girbaud. He used to take me shopping and let me buy shit for my girlfriend and never said he bought the stuff when she was around. Many of his qualities of sharing and giving I began to have in my life. Big D had access to a lot of things. Guns, drugs etc. Now I had access to even more negative things than before. Big D was smart. He pumped his own drugs. He had workers but didn't really want that. At times he refused to give me work because he said he would flip more if he moved it himself. So now I am moving with him. Going everywhere and introducing him to all my dudes from Queens. He and Cormega knew each other from the Bronx when they were little and Mega hung with Ocean and Super and the rest of my Q.B. crew at the time. So everything just clicked. They were in Q.B. doing their one, two things and I was doing the same. By this time, me and the Q.B. crew had grouped up with dudes from another block out in the projects and became one crew called "The Goodfellas" This added my man Trevor, Spank, Karate, Skins, Beef stick, Germ and a few others. We were deep and ready for war against any crew. My team held down the 41st side of Twelfth Street and nobody could hustle on that block period!

One day Ocean gave me 350 dollars to give Big D to pick him up a new .380 gun. I went home that night and my mother had locked me out of the house. I got upset and rang the bell. When she opened the door she started asking me, where were you? What were you doing? Why are your eyes red? Why were you drinking? This infuriated me because I didn't drink back then so as I brushed past her I mumbled bullshit under my breath. She followed behind me to my room. When I turned around, she asked me what I was carrying in my pocket. I was like 'damn' to myself because it was Ocean's bread for the gun. It was only $350 but looked like a thousand because of the little bills. I said "What? It's Ocean's money." She pulled it out and said "Hell no we are going to his house now and it better be his." I was sick. My mom wanted to tell his mother that he had this type of money which she thought was a lot but it wasn't. We went to his house and it was about one in the morning. Luckily he was outside and they sent me to go find him. I went to 12th street where he was hustling and told him the situation. Nigga was tight!! He had reason to be. We walked back to his crib and told the story that it was Draws' money. This is a guy from the block that Ocean came from who sold drugs. Ocean's mom seemed like she believed him but my mom kept pressing on the issue. Things calmed down and my mother and I went home. Within a few days, Ocean was sent to Texas to live with family. That man was sending death threats to me, he was heated. It's funny now, but I was upset too because he was my ace dude when I went down to Q.B. I mean I loved Los, Super, Cliffy, Trevor, Spank, etc. but Ocean was from when we were three years old. Meanwhile me and Big D kept having fun getting money, looking good, and saving up to get the car he wanted. To me that was the last step to being an official dealer. Having that car and a few dollars in the stash. I don't remember exactly when I made the decision but one was made that if I get $10,000 and a car I was out of the game. I felt that was enough. The only thing I didn't factor in was what I would do next after I got to that stage of the game. Where would I work? What skills did I have? I had a lot of general knowledge, but in life you need special skills to really get ahead. Knowing a little about a lot of different things might keep you in fruitless conversations, but in the real world it wasn't that beneficial. I guess the only specialty skill I was learning was with hands on experience at that!

Big D was a people's person and so was I. So with the best quality of drugs at the time, and with his people skills, it was no problem raking in the dough. I remember one time when I was attending Queens Vocational High School I saw a few of my friends from Southside and they were robbing dudes from the school down the block which was Aviation high school. They had leathers and a few dollars. So I went back down there with them. It was me and my man Sharwin from Sutphin and 121, and this other Black dude from

Brooklyn. We saw a dude that was heavy on the jewels from Aviation. I figured 'Jackpot!' We ran down on him and stuck him up. Went straight to Jamaica Avenue, pawned the chains, bracelets and rings and bought plenty of gear and footwear. Even brought my man Nikko from Hammels a few items and he wasn't even down with the robbery. It was a Friday so the weekend was sweet. That Monday came and there were problems when I got off the train and was walking towards the school. I saw my man who did the robbery walking a few blocks ahead. I didn't call him I just walked behind him figuring I would see him in school. When we got to the block of the school, I saw the principal with two cops grab my man. They were talking to him about the robbery. I just kept walking into the school and they didn't stop me. Once in the classroom, I was called to the principal's office. I hated that Mr. Serber motherfucker. He tried to be on my back a lot but I always had my shit in order. Well not this time. I got there and they had my man Sharwin and was addressing him. He acted like he had no idea what they were talking about. A robbery where, what? He was saying. My other man who did it with us didn't come to school this day. So we sat there until the bitch nigga that got robbed, who was a stick up kid himself, came into the office and looked at us. When he left I was sure he said it wasn't us but the principal came back in and said that he informed our parents because we were going to jail. Crazy shit, dudes that were doing crime have always been snitching, ain't shit changed. So this was my first time really going through some serious shit. That's when you would be in central booking 3days. If you didn't see a judge in one night, they would transport you to a precinct with cells to sleep then bring you back to court the next day and so forth. Me and my man kicked it all night for two days in those pens.

He was going out with a girl from Queensbridge that went to our school that I liked. He said he wasn't travelling out there to see her from Jamaica and he didn't care if I fucked with her. I said 'don't play nigga,' he said 'whatever.' Probably would have scooped her anyway once summer came but it was good that he was cool with it. I did scoop her and she ended up being my son's mother. Keesha Wright. We have a great son that graduated from St. John's University. See how you have a bad situation and make something good from it. Well we caught the robbery charge and my bail was seven hundred and fifty dollars. That was too much for my blood, I had no money, I didn't save, and I was a half assed crook that pumped for sneakers and gear. I didn't call my mother though, I always felt that if you go against what your parents teach you as a kid and break their rules then handle your problems on your own. Period!! So that's what I planned on doing. It was the first time I went to Rikers Island. I was sixteen. The island was really wild but I was the type to ask a lot of questions to the older guys in my hood about jail and prison because they all went a few times, so I knew what to expect. Not going to front, I was fresh from that Friday robbery and I put a little dirt on my new Reeboks pumps. Those joints were like $200 back then. Did not want to look too fresh because it would attract more attention than I knew if I was ready for. Shit popped off as soon as I got to the pens. Some dude that had the same color that I had on had beef so when one guy told the other to cut the guy in the red and black I thought they were referring to me. They weren't though and the guy that was told to pop off didn't do it to the kid. He told him "damn boy how you gonna come through knowing you got beef? I ain't gonna do anything but believe you better get bailed out before you run into their dudes" referring to the guys that told him to cut the kid. After that, everything seemed to cool down. The officers were making fun of how young I looked and said my mom should beat me when I got home. Big D bailed me out and when I got out about 2:30 in the morning, he and my sister were waiting for me on the island. Real love with no strings attached. He didn't care that it wasn't drug related he just wanted his man out. In hindsight, a lot of dudes can credit much of the helping hand I gave out to the street to the way this guy moved with me in the street. I kept robbing and hustling as usual.

I went to court on Sutphin Blvd. on 89th Avenue in Jamaica Queens. It was known as Suffering Blvd. The court was known to be tougher on people that went there compared to if you went to court on Queens Blvd., which is the main building. Not sure how true that was because I had seen guys get hung in both buildings. I ended up catching another robbery case in that damn school while fighting the first case. Me and my man Ill-Will from Q.B. caught a good Vic together. This is the guy Nas shouts out. His best friend that ended up getting killed. He was in my school and we used to rob people together also. He was a wild dude and really funny. I got knocked off first and the police told me that they didn't believe that we robbed the guy. They said they had to go through the formalities. They let me go and gave me a few days to come back for an interview but told me to bring Will back so they could close the case. I wasn't sure if they were lying but I was just happy to leave the precinct that day. I found Will on 10th street in Q.B. a few days later and told him what they said. He too was skeptical and he also had two open robbery cases. Damn we sound like some Brooklyn crooks! We decided to go in on the day they told us to. The day just happened to be Wills birthday. The whole time at the precinct the cops were being really nice, each giving us food and letting us watch video music box but they assured us that we would be going home after a few hours of waiting. They came back and said they had to send us through the system, but we would be out of the system within 2 hours. We were sick, figuring we were tricked. Not tricked, because we really did think we would get arrested but we wanted to believe them. I had an open case and he had two. This would finalize our trip to prison. There was no way we wouldn't have to pay some type of debt to society for this. They kept assuring us that it was procedure, and we would get let go. So we were arrested and booked. They said we were getting something called a "343" which will get our case dismissed. We sat in booking like every other crook in there but after about fifteen hours they called our names, they opened the cells and let us out the back door. Oh God we were happy. Charges were dismissed, never had to see a judge and we were free just like the police said. May be the first and last time a cop ever was honest to me. Hey I guess they aren't all bad after all. Me and Sharwin made a deal with the bitch ass nigga on our other case to pay him for his jewels so he would say he made a mistake. We told him he would get half before he went to court and dropped the charges and half after. He agreed. He partly agreed because he was a crook that knew he was out of line for telling the cops in the first place. Well my man paid him the first half but you know he got deaded on the second half. The charges were dropped. He must be crazy if he thought I was gonna pay him my half.

Big D ended up getting knocked for a few charges of drugs in Queens and an assault and robbery in the Bronx. When he left; he gave me about 125gs and told me to get busy. This was the start of being a boss. He either went in late '89 or early '90 and that 125gs seemed like a damn kilo to me. I was definitely overwhelmed. I was used to just pumping light packs. I was the type to never owe anyone and never want to let people down so as I moved this much crack I saw it was too much for me at one time. So I finished all the work. I gave the money to his sister, I told her to tell him that I cannot fuck with that but here is all the money. Never wanted to fuck up on a dude that did so much for me. So after that I got a few grams and started slow. Before I knew it I was clicking and had developed a great relationship with fiends from being with Big D and my man Joe. Joe was doing his thing over all this time also on the other side of the projects. At one point all the other G's were in prison in my hood, G-Man, Raymond, Devin, Jayvon, Mike, U.V, Majestic and a few others. Point blank, it wasn't too many times that they were all home at the same time. So when any of them came home they never fronted on me but I damn sure wasn't telling them they couldn't eat. We all deserved it. I knew I could out-hustle all of them dudes. I probably became partners with each one of them at one point in time because dudes knew I was thorough, young, smart and had clientele. I didn't care about having it all but I was eating. At one time Devin and I were down. At one time me, Jayvon, Debo and Mece were down. We were called the Four Horsemen had rhinestone hats big chains with matching bracelets. G-Man and I were down together and so were me and Raymond. At one time or another I was partners with all the guys I used to hustle for. Now that's a promotion in the game! There were some other players in my hood, Hi-C, my friend and confidant Chuck, A-Wol, JP and Butch who was the youngest person in charge. Very sharp in the mind can turn a Nickel into a bag of money. Out of all the guys down my way my QB crew gravitated to G-Man the most. They loved him. Always wanted him around with us. He was a tough cookie. He also was known to be getting money and being wild. He became a member of the Goodfellas gang. We had blocks by this time. We done ran one of the biggest dealers from Q.B. out the hood.

This dude was getting paper. He had the truck and BMWs and a Benz and big chains and everything a nigga should have. That's one thing I admired more about Q.B. than the dealers around my way. They all had hot cars and jewelry and they were just what you pictured when you pictured a drug dealer that had success. How much cash they were sitting on I don't know. They looked the part period! Shit, you might not have shit but if I believe you got it, I am striving for that number. So if you're fronting, it doesn't matter because I can grab and stash what I "think" you have. Yeah, my man Trev had beef with the kid and the two of them had a fight and Cormega jumped in for Trev which led to like everything else, GUNPLAY. I got the call down my way and suited up and got my gun to hurry down the block to put the plan in order to do whatever we were gonna do. At this time, my man Justice from my hood was hustling down in Q.B. with this guy named Fun. So it was a coincidence that when I came out of the building he was standing there and he had heard about the fight and knew it would be gunplay but I didn't want him to know that I was involved just in case anyone got killed. The shit was crazy, we had about 14 dudes ready to ride. Trev demanded that type of love; he was a boss in his own right. We decided to surround the block and come in from all the exits. Not too smart of a move, considering that we could hit each other in the crossfire but that was our choice. I had a nickel plated .38 and my man Spank had the pump shot gun. He and I covered the 21st street entrance. Everyone else went to whatever entrances they wanted to go to. Shit was crazy because when the shit went down it was popping like crazy. It sounded like the Fourth of July.

53

The block was dark so I told Spank to wait before we ran in. As about 200 rounds were let off, I saw a dude with a pump, backing out of the block. I didn't know if he was with us or not. I asked Spank "who that" he just ran into the block and let that pump loose. I came right behind him and started dumping. After it was done, one nigga was torn up and we actually thought he was dead but he wasn't. The police lit the block up like Christmas for hours investigating. We were across the street on the roof watching and waiting to see what the damage was. I passed my gun to Trev and told him "I was never here." He said of course, and I walked the backstreets and went back to my hood. There were a lot of shootings that were the same way. Our crew stood together and would let them hammers go in a second. Everywhere we went we were gripped up. If we had 10 niggas we had 10 guns. It was part of the damn outfit, and at this point we were getting money. Trev and his part of the crew were probably spending 15 stacks a week, and Super and his part of the crew might have been spending 10 or 12. Now remember this, years ago grams were way cheaper so 10 to 15 stacks got you plenty of coke and the profit was enormous especially since it was getting broke down to dimes. So after this shoot out with the kid, we stayed on his ass, we popped his man up and were hunting for him. So one day we thought we had a sighting of him. It was myself, G-Man, Trev and Ocean standing at the phone booth on the north side of Queensbridge. We all had about 100 cracks and a gun on us. We were in front of the dude building. I don't know if someone called or it was just a coincidence but the police came towards us from every direction. It was on. Everyone was running their separate ways. I ran and dropped into this southern restaurant that my man from Mobb Deep's family owned and passed my shit to my man Joe Shan. Trev was a fat dude that ran down 21st towards my P.J.s which was crazy. Ocean and G-Man ran the long way down 40th avenue. Police chased the both of them, they were moving fast. Halfway down the block, G-Man decided to cut back and try to run back towards Ravenswood. It was a weird move. Ocean kept running but the police car was about to cut him off as he got to the corner. As they approached he pulled out his Mac 11 and pointed it at the police car and they backed off and he was able to dip into the hood and got away. G-Man wasn't that lucky, they chased him and he jumped over a barb wire fence into some tall weeds, he had to take his leather off to protect himself from the wire. So they found the coat with the drugs and knew he was in those weeds. He hid for so long I thought he got out of there without being spotted. They brought helicopters and all and still couldn't find him. Eventually they brought the K-9 and gave his jacket to smell and brought it in the weeds. That nigga gave up. He didn't want that dog to bite him. So now he was knocked. You couldn't tell us that the dude didn't call the cops on us and we wanted blood. I went and told G-Man brother, and his brother wanted to go back to Q.B. that night. I told him it was too hot but he insisted. So we got with their man at the time who became a great friend to me, Tom who had a tinted Jeep Cherokee. We were circling looking for this dude. There was no sign of him. We figured out where he could be because his black 1990 five series was parked by the bar in the hood. There was no sign of him though. I told Tom to leave but J.P. said fuck that, lets tear that whip up he will come out. I said fuck it. We pulled up beside his car and got on both sides and swiss cheesed it. Everyone was running from the corner either scared from the shots or didn't want anyone to think they had anything to do with it. I didn't give a fuck either way because there was a prior issue with this dude maybe a year before when he fronted on me and I wanted payback.

Prior to this beef his brother and man were in my hood at the chicken spot and were getting out of line with G-Man's girl at the time. So Raymond and a few others ended up fucking them niggas up and sending shots at them and ran them out of my hood. So this guy was used to seeing me with my dudes in Q.B. so when he was coming through looking for dudes for what they did he was jumping out on dudes sending threats around. One day he said to me, "You little man if I can't catch up to them I am gonna see you." I was like "WHAT!" went straight to Ocean to get the HAMMER and see what was up. Ocean was cool with the dude and addressed the issue and he said it had nothing to do with me. I hated that dude for that. So hitting him or his shit I didn't give a fuck. At this time we were coming into our own, we were ready for war anytime and anyplace. We were buying jewelry now and I got a couple of dollars saved. Even went and bought a BMW from an auction. My man Jayvon brought me to get it. The bidding was really fast I couldn't keep up. I ended up buying an old ass BMW about 10 years old. This car is what most people think was my first car but I actually brought a Burgundy Jeep first that was tough but I had a few bad situations with it and sold it. I told my man Andre to get me a radio for a

Cherokee, he said bet and I came out the next day and my window was broken. This nigga stole my fucking radio to sell it to me! How crazy was that? He didn't know it was my car he broke into. We went everywhere in that orange BMW and mad people had jokes. They called it the car from the movie "Marked for Death" with the Jamaican posse in it. Little did they know that these were stepping stones in my life to show I could save a dollar and be responsible and be a boss. My cars went from those to a Honda Civic to a Toyota Camry then I got knocked off. Caught a few cases for drugs. My name was getting; big our crew's name was getting big too. From the masked shooting we did in Astoria projects to the big Ravenswood shooting to the many shoot outs between our crew and Draws who at one time was on our team and at the end of the day, he was one of the realest gangsters from Q.B. Very well respected in the streets. We were running up in people's cribs and pulling them out of their houses at gunpoint. Robbing dudes in the hood, we really became terrors. We had guns with infrared beams on them and used to play by waiting at night and putting the beam on people's heads and face. Mind you all of this is before we were men still in the teenage years.

I already moved my baby's mother from QB to an apartment in Corona, Queens. After the shooting in Astoria we were anti-Astoria. So one day a dude was in Q.B. seeing a girl and he was from Astoria. He had the big chain on and Ocean decided to stick him. Homey faked a move and got robbed and shot. Now Ocean did that because we didn't fuck with Astoria but also he wanted the chain. I didn't find out about what happened for days. When I saw him I asked where the chain came from and he said jokingly "don't worry about it," so I left it alone. We all were heavy by '91 anyway. I was still the only one in our immediate crew driving, and our other man 40. Then days later we had an incident where some dudes had said Ocean and Mega aint shit without Ice. Oh, God why did they say that? As me, Ocean, and Mega were boasting about ourselves to each other and I mentioned that, one of the kids that said it happened to come though. Mega called him and started to push up on the kid. We were on the hill and it was crowded up there. While the guy was responding, Ocean broke a bottle and cut the nigga and then we just destroyed the dude and his man. A regular day in the damn ghetto for us.

Right after that my sister had an incident where some dude pulled a shotgun and pointed at her while she was pregnant with my nephew. No way will that happen! It was the upstairs neighbor family over some bullshit. So I saw my mother and sister outside arguing with the guy's family but the dude wasn't there. I was standing in the next building with my sister's baby's father and his cousin, Jay and Russell. As their argument got louder the guy who supposedly pulled the shotgun came out and sure enough he had a duffle bag with him. He was talking crazy so I decided to walk out there. It was a sunny afternoon and kids were in the park and a bunch of women were arguing, I didn't like that the dude came out talking. So as I was walking toward them with Jay and Russell, the guy's sister says "he right there" pointing towards me and my dudes. I don't know what she thought but we were HOLDING. This dude picks the duffle up and unzips it and motions to run towards us. My mother and sister were telling us to run. See this is where I ask myself how far will I go? I sent shots at the man while he was standing in the direction of where my family was standing. My sister could have been shot or my mother. That would have been sick and ironic since I ended up doing worse than the guy that I was looking for did. Decision-making is everything to me. One bad move and you are done. We had already stopped because there was too much drama with the yelling but this fool started running at us. Jay pulled out first, which the whole world saw. He took a shot at the guy then his gun jammed. This dude dropped. I thought he was dead. I ran through the building and came out through the back. Jay and his cousin went one way and I went the other. Police came and the snitching began. Nobody even got shot but the police wanted me knocked off. So they got the family to say it was me. Which it was but don't snitch. This dude came running at us, we found out he only had a sledge hammer in the bag. Fool ass nigga. So the police were looking for me and when I told Ocean he said they went to his house for something but didn't know why. So we decided to get into the rentals, which they kept and go to Great Adventure and Atlantic City until we found out what was going on. This shit is insane as I write these words. It's one thing if you got into something crazy in your life once or maybe twice and most people only get one shot before they are arrested or killed but all that I am saying, is up to and before Ocean went to Jail in '92. Maybe if my father was still around he could have helped me end my life of crime way back then, but he wasn't. Still don't want to point the finger at him though, Just a thought.

I paid dues I lived through three decades of street life. Never having a chance to exhale until now while I am sitting in jail. Not complaining just want to educate. I'm not saying what is right or wrong but we must have been stupid or thought it was a game when the police was on us for a shooting I did and either a shooting he did plus robbery and or the assault we pulled on the hill and we decided to go get on roller coasters and try to get into the casinos. At this point we were immune to crime but punishment started to come to us one by one. I was a little upset with my sister because while I was laying low I told her to convince the neighbors that it wasn't me shooting and she kept telling me that she wasn't saying shit to them and fuck them, etc. I told her that their fear would get them to stay snitching. My sister is stubborn so she was being very difficult on the matter so I decided to just see how shit played out. She eventually talked to the lady but she waited until the lady came to her. They wanted no problems I guess. My man Jay was ultimately arrested for the shooting which he later beat months down the line. I dodged another bullet. The story of my life. Ocean on the other hand was arrested on his shooting and charged with robbery and attempted murder. The case was strong but not too strong. He had a 25k bail. We immediately hit the streets and got the money up and bailed him out. The kid who was shot was supposed to be some square and that was why he was telling. To this day I am not sure but what I was sure of is that we were gonna press the dude to drop the charges. We found out that the kid's brother name was Shawn who was in the street doing things. So we decided to find him and talk to him to handle this situation. This dude wasn't too cooperative acting as if he couldn't tell his brother what to do. I am not sure whether we offered to pay or they asked for money for them to drop the charges, but it was the deal that never happened. We decided on something else.

Me, Super, Trev and Cliffy went to River Park. This is the big park behind the projects where the parties for kid's BBQ, park jams and whatever else went down. We decided to draw straws between the four of us and the short straw gets a shot in the leg. If this ain't crazy I don't what is! After the person gets shot we will drop them at the hospital and he would say that the brother of the guy Ocean shot is the one who shot one of us. We figured if there are cross complaints, dude would fear for his brother and want to end this faggot shit he was doing. The straws were drawn and my man Cliffy caught the short one, damn. Well it had to be one of us. We also drew straws to see who would be the shooter because no one was anxious to pop our own man. Who the shooter was don't matter but it was done. He was hit right over the knee; luckily we almost fucked this plan up. He hit the ground like a ton of bricks but kept saying, "I love yall niggas, I love yall niggas." We picked him up and dropped him off at the hospital and watched to see how shit played out. What we thought was a great crime turned to be not so perfect and it had the police looking at us like we would do anything on the streets. If they will shoot one of their own and he allowed it, what wont they do? The big detective at the time was "C". This dude was a Goodfella hunter. He took Cormega down for a robbery the year before this that he didn't do and he blew trial and caught a 5 to 15 year jail sentence. So at this point we were down a few dudes. This clown eventually arrested my man Trev and Beef Stick for two attempted murders also. He wanted everyone in our crew. He also was the cop that had me for the shooting in my hood when the lady was grazed. Anyway this fucking officer arrests the dude we tried to frame and then met him at the arraignment and testified to the judge that he doesn't believe he did the shooting and to release him ROR and shit. The judge kindly did fucking ROR for a shooting assault when the complaint said he did it. Fucking crazy. We kept the pressure on trying now to find the brother to pop his ass.

One day I was going to one of my workers' house and saw the dude's car parked in my hood. Myself and my little worker waited by his car but he never came. We went, got the gun and went to the house we thought he was at but no one answered. I had little dudes smash his car up with bats. This dude came to the window of the apartment he was in yelling and talking shit but never came down. One day we all went to court with Ocean and his lawyer said that Ocean was gonna be re-arrested and the rest of us might be also for tampering with a witness. We went to the courtroom; they snatched Ocean and re-arrested him. That same bitch-ass detective. The rest of us broke out so we wouldn't get snatched. Ocean had to end up taking 4 to 12 years in prison for this shooting. By 1992 a lot of my crew had either did bids or were doing them. G-Man had came home because he had shock. Big D was still in, Ocean gone, Beef Stick was released and went on the run, and one of the wildest dudes we fucked with Spank was gone. He was just wild by nature and he was loyal. Him and Ocean did bids together for about seven years straight. Spank got jammed up on a carjacking. Spank and me and our man Junior went and did a carjacking in Brooklyn. There was a situation that we needed to handle but we needed a car to do it and I had a car but we couldn't roll to the shooting in it. So we got on the Grand Central Parkway looking for a victim. This is when the Lexus just came out. We tried to follow one but the car was too fast and we didn't want to speed to keep up because we either had a Mac 11 or a Tech 9 in the car with us. We were getting real deep on the highway so we decided to exit and turn around. As soon as we got off the exit we saw a brand new Maxima double parked at the corner. That was good enough for us. Those joints were hot at the time. The round joints when they first came out in '90 or '91. Anyway, there was a Spanish man on the pay phone and someone sitting in his passenger seat. Junior was driving because he was an excellent driver under pressure. Spank and I jumped out of the car and walked to the door. I opened the door and tried to pull the man out of the passenger seat.

He was screaming and yelling and pulling away. His friend dropped the phone and ran towards us. Spank spun the machine gun on him, and he turned and ran. Then I yanked the man out of the car, Spank pistol-whipped him and we got in and drove off while Junior drove the other car which was my damn Honda. I was praying no one got the plates. Spank loved that shit but I just did it because we had a plan to pop someone up and we needed a car. We pulled over and checked the car out when we got off back at our exit, Hoyt Avenue. We took a tape from my car, popped it in and drove to park the stolen car until we needed it. I thought our cover was blown because on the way down 21st street, we saw our man Spunk a.k.a Hype at the light and I hoped he didn't notice the car because he had the same one. He didn't see us so went on our way. My man Spunk is in N.C doing life, one love my nigga. He was one of the best to ever do it at a young age and one of the people I admired and set my drug dealer dreams after.

So as far as the situation went, the guy we were looking for, wasn't coming around for some reason. The shit we wanted to do was gonna be done on the hill in the daylight. The plan was simple:

pull up on the guy with masks on in a brand new car, and get him. It's sick how we talk about violence like it's a regular thing. Shit, back then you couldn't blame rap music; this is when Biggie, Nas, Jay Z and Pac were just starting. Before Snoop. It was just things we did in the projects. Anyway, we figured everybody had beef with dudes from other places and it wouldn't trace back to us. The dude we was gonna get was a real dude but he needed to go because we kept having ongoing beef with him. After a few days with no sight of him, this dude Spank decided to start driving the damn car around like it was his. I was pissed the fuck off! I don't just commit these type of crimes like car-jacking for fun. I had a big argument with him. I told him that right now it was hot, people now know we driving stolen damn cars so the mask with the car might trace back to us if we tried it. He didn't get it. He said he would steal us a different car then we could still do the work. I thought, 'No Spank the plan is weak now whether we use one stolen car or another.' He went and stole the car anyway from someone who had their car double parked in Harlem with my man Tuffy and ended up in a car chase with police. He was caught and arrested. The early nineties were rough. My whole Q.B. crew went down, well not all of us.

Ocean 4 to 12, Mega 5-15, Spank not sure but did seven. Forty 2-4, Cliffy 3-9 for a shooting on New Year's Eve. The police ended up in a chase with him and he let loose shots in the building to back them down and they shot him in his back. Super laid up for eighteen months for a murder until he beat it. Then there was the infamous shooting that we did on the south side of Queensbridge. We kept beef with these dudes. They didn't get into as much shit as us and weren't as deep as us but I respected them. As a matter of fact, I liked them dudes. Let's be clear, most of these situations up to now were not my immediate beef, but I roll with my crew and they did for me so it was what it was.

Back in the '90s, guns were everywhere. My man Trev had a cousin that sold guns and we had them all. Glocks when they first came out, Mac 11, Tech 9, .380, .38, .44, .45, and 8 shot pumps with pistol grips and the 10 mm. The list goes on, we could of also gotten grenades but who was holding that in their crib? Not I. Anyway I believe it was around Thanksgiving and we were gonna have a big dinner at my man Forever's house because the crew was our family. Some of my niggas' parents were fiends and we decided to let the girls in our crew cook. Tiny, Nicole, Hope, Miesha, Tawana, Niqua and the rest of them. Somewhere along that week, these dudes came on 12th street and were shooting at niggas. They had our home girls running off the block, and my man Ramone who was on crutches already for shooting himself in the leg by accident, had to dive out the way and ended up breaking his leg again. The girls called us and it was on from there. The two problems we had were that Tiny, one of our homies, was fuckin' with a dude from that block who she eventually had a baby with. So she wanted to warn the dude. Also our man Forty had cousins there that he wanted to make sure weren't outside. First off, one of his cousins was one of the targets and he knew that. How the fuck can they go warn their people, and think we will have the drop? It just can't happen. Forty and I got into it to where I took back a Benzi box radio I gave him for his car, and told him to go fuck with them dudes. Eventually our arguments got straightened out. He really just wanted that radio back. I cannot really remember if we let Tiny tell the nigga or not, but we rode hard over there, eight deep coming from the two back exits tearing the block to shreds. There was only three people out that night on the block. When the fire stopped all three were down, but only two got hit up. The main target dodged the bullets. Of course the innocent dude in their crew, was hit a couple of times. He was in critical condition for a while. He didn't snitch and the dude that used to be in gunplay let his sister put niggas away for a long time. His sister took the stand and said she saw Trev and Beef Stick shooting but didn't know the other shooters. How though, if everyone wore masks? She said after the shooting we came on the hill to use the phone and Trevor took his mask off and she saw him. Bullshit! And if you let your family rat, nigga you a rat! He could have prevented it. Well that's what I think. Beef Stick got a 9 to 18 and Trev caught a 7 to 14. Last but not least it was my turn. Through all this I am still doing my one two in my hood. I was on my fourth whip now. A blue Toyota Camry. At this point in time I always had used cars but nothing less than 2 years old so if its '92 my car was probably '90 or '91. Now I started catching drug charges, one with my little brother Dash who rides with me to the end and is also a co-defendant on my case now. And another with my man Hi-C who I grew up with and it will go off topic to tell about the shooting in the Bronx where he lives. I caught probation for 2 sales, then after 5 months on probation I caught another case and took a year on Rikers Island. By October

1993 we were all in. The girls in our crew were visiting on a regular. I moved my baby moms to a crib in Corona and paid the bills for the whole eight months before I went to do the bid. I tried to be responsible as a father because mine was not available. I loved the life, I loved my crew. We were young and reckless.

There was the shoot out around Easter at the Carnival in Brooklyn or when a nigga say they gonna pick you up, they drove through the block doing forty having people jumping out of the way to stop in front of your building. Life was wild. We were institutionalized to the streets. So I ask up until '93 were we the same type of dudes? I don't know. I probably don't regret my actions only because I got away with them. We were people leading by example doing crime. Most of us knew people that got the jobs in banks and went to college and worked at civil service jobs but I was blinded by the fun and the thrills of showing people I was "wit it" or a "tough guy'. I am blessed to still be here because of all the violence but believe me this wasn't an isolated situation. This was many people's reality.

My bid was cool. I kept in touch with Super who was fighting his murder case. I kept in touch with Ocean and Spank who were about a year and a half into their stretches. I ran into my man Boobie who was living in BK but used to live on my block in Ravenswood. He was down on a gun beef. It was great seeing him and we became extremely close. He was a year or two younger than me but he wasn't young minded. Just a sucker for love. His girl was driving him crazy, so crazy that he would give me his phone time. He had 9-10 click, I had 7-9. Yeah, this was before they started the twenty one-minute shit in the jails. As a matter of fact it was just being put in jails while I was doing my time but we never experienced it back then. My visit game was crazy. Three a week and never missed one. Money on the books and I was in Queens House of Detention working so I saw plenty of dudes either coming to court from the island or coming through new admissions. Our officer used to let us play the halls. It's different now. I think we only had to pop off on dudes two times. Spanish dudes started acting crazy over the TV when they got deep; even pulled a razor I had to hem one up, then his Latin King homies handled him. One other issue was with this giant dude named what else…Tiny! This dude was trying to intimidate us about the phone. He didn't like that slot time started at 5.30. Get the Fuck outta here Tiny, everyone was cool with that. One day shit got really heated and we geared up, got the razor, batteries in the sock, broomsticks etc., and whipped this nigga out something terrible. It was me, my man Boobie, our homie Unique and a few others. Unique used to tell me he was the 50 Cent from BK's cousin. Shit was wild because when police rushed the house, I had his blood on my shirt and Boobie passed me one of the ones he had on. Everyone got packed up and shipped to the island except me. They acted like they were arresting dudes but they didn't.

The next morning I hear someone talking about the phone was his and this and that bullshit. It was fucking Tiny. They brought him back and he was talking crazy. I locked out and was trying to slip into the dayroom to get the razor when Tiny looked out of his cell. I was a little nervous but showed no fear. He started yelling, "CO, CO what is he still doing here?" In my head I said, "What?" this nigga is crazy. He was going so crazy the "A" officers moved him out of the house to the other side. Damn, never let the size fool ya, that nigga was pussy. Let me say this, jail is nowhere to be or to glamorize but if you put yourself knee-deep into the game, accept your fate. Don't break, don't tell under any circumstances. Play by the rules that the street made. Do not cheat if someone else in the game cheats. Stay with your own principles, live and die by your decisions. My man Shameek said to me one day, "If you are ready to kill be ready to die". That shit has always stuck with me, and you have choices. You don't have to commit crimes, it's not a must. There are plenty of other options if you apply yourself, educate yourself. Becoming a top drug dealer is slim to none. I don't even know if I should call my life a success from this game. There are higher levels than what I saw, but I have to live with my regrets.

Now we gonna get into these mid-nineties to the early 2000's. At one time I didn't think that life could get any better, this is the era of Snoop and Biggie, Nas, Mobb Deep and Jay-Z. I came home from jail focused and ready to get money. I was way past my dream of getting 10 grand and a car and fall back out the game. Shit I made 16K while I was in jail. My man G-Man dropped 500 a week to my home girl and one of my best friends Netfa. Her brother and I used to get money together back in the days then after a small beef and a shooting I did, the people we had beef with caught up to him and knocked him out and gave him a crazy shiner, that was it for him. He told me, "after this pack I QUIT." I was like "DAMN because of one beating nigga, we fucked many people up." Hey it was probably good because I'd rather have a nigga back out then snitch somewhere down the line. So anyway, by '94, G-Man, myself, Raymond and man Devin had the neighborhood for a few years. My man Joe and a few others also was doing them but our block was super clicking 24-hours a day complete with look-outs, shifts, and managers. When I got home I was sitting on stacks and had my income clicking from the block. I sold my Camry and still had my crib with Keesha in Corona. Shit was about to get better though. Before I got home in June of '94 my man Big D dropped. He was gone since 1990 and did 4 of his 2-6. I really loved that guy and wanted to show I appreciated everything he taught and showed me. I went to visit him when he was away in Cayuga and me and his brother ended up having a big fight on the floor. He was telling Big D how I was getting money and I should be blessing him. On a visit one day my home girl Netfa told me that Big D was home. I was like, "Damn, how he look?" She said he was fine. We discussed what I should do for him. Remind you I was still locked up at the time. I decided I would let her take him shopping and give him two thousand cash and buy him a Movado watch. They were hot back then. In those years before I went to jail, I had Gucci, Fendi and Movado and a Tag Heuer watch. I always had a nice chain, a bracelet and a diamond ring sometimes. G-Man had the most jewels out of my Ravenswood crew but everyone had something nice in that department. She did it and he was happy I had done that for him. He didn't really fuck with G-Man, Raymond and Devin like that so he mostly stayed in the BX on the come home. There wasn't any beef he was more my friend and Big Joe.

I had big plans for when I got home that June of '94, but shit could not go as planned on the streets. A week before coming home I made a call to my man Forever's house which was like the headquarters for our crew. I was upbeat about dropping but they informed me that they just got into some new beef again!! I was tight, I wanted to get money. I had plans but this was part of the game. I ask what happened, they told me that a couple of dudes we had beef with who'd got shot during those beefs, came down to our hood fronting. There were words exchanged at the store and they were with a dude who was fronting real hard. This dude had just got some type of settlement and brought a Q-45 and it made him think he was a goon. I don't know if guns were drawn but whatever happened was enough for G-Man to borrow Big D's .45, and him and Raymond rode down to Q.B. looking for them. They got out there and ending up parking somewhere. While they sat in Raymond's car, the Q-45 pulled on the side of Raymond's car window, rolled down the window and started shooting into Raymond's car. G-Man didn't return fire. The .45 he had gotten from Big D had a double safety that G-Man wasn't aware of so when he went to shoot, it didn't fire. Luckily, neither of my comrades were hit that day, but I was coming home to beef most definitely. I told them I was with whatever but let me breathe for a second, let's not go looking for them right away but if we see them we will handle it. They agreed. I guess they were looking out for me since I was coming home fresh. I dropped home in June. Perfect timing, Summer time.

We were having a tournament in my projects. Everyone was pleased to see me, I was the talk of the goddamn town. I was loving it. I immediately hit my block and seen my crew. It was Peanut, Dash, Vic, Nisha, Lamont and a few others. Everyone had a shift, Nisha had gotten fired while I was in jail for whatever reason and I told her I would handle that for her when I got home because she was really down for the team. She was one of the first people I had brought from another land to hustle for us when we had the 24-hour block clicking. There was Joe Shan, Skins and Big Germ, Shanel, Vic, Tee-tee, Donna, Rakia, Arabia, all of which was from Q.B. They all hustled at different times and years but they were all part of my team in Ravenswood. Cannot forget my man Shawn Perdue from AQ. Five days after I got home from jail I went and brought the four door Pathfinder. Shit was hot, there I was barely 21 and home from jail 5 days and got the '92 Pathfinder, even though it was '94, my man Spunk had one before I went to jail and I loved it and wanted it back in those days. All cars were bought straight cash. Shit, I didn't even have a license back then. That summer was popping and I was at every event popping bottles. We would go deep and buy 10 bottles of Moet. Prices were different back then and they only sold White

Star and Dom P at many spots. Everyone was listening to Snoop's album but Mobb Deep had dropped and was crazy and Biggie's shit was bootlegged and Nas was hot. On our side we had all the music because so many people had record deals. I fucked with all the rap groups. Mobb Deep was my little mans and they were from the block that my GoodFella crew controlled. Nas went to school with me and we were cool, girls liked him and they liked me. He was also a close friend to a dude who used to hustle for my man Big D named Smiley. Nas used to come to our hood sometimes with Ill-Will, they all was crew.

When Mobb-deep shot their 'Shook-Ones' video, I lent Havoc my Pathfinder to use in the video. He's in the backseat while I'm driving if you have that video in the stash. I also loaned out two Avirex leathers for their crew to wear in the 'Hell-on-Earth' video because they wanted everyone to be looking the same. I got a good look in that video and also a light shot in their 'Survival of the Fittest' video. These dudes were hot and there was no denying it. We rolled deep to clubs and shut a lot of them down. They were rowdy, young-acting youths, while Nas hung out with the more mature dudes from the hood but could get just as rowdy. So I came home

shining getting money like I never missed a beat and now I was

growing hungry for money, now it's an addiction. By this time my

son's mother and I had broken up and G-Man and I had two

apartments that his lawyer owned on Merrick and Linden Blvd in

Jamaica Queens. He moved and shortly after and I took both

apartments. He probably left because of all the traffic of, people I

used to bring around. A lot of women and sometimes workers so we

could fuck bitches. By this time a lot of dudes in the street started

shifting their energy to music but I stayed focused and tried to get to

the top and fast!

Well the Fourth of July came of '94 which is my man's

Dash's birthday. It seemed like we always got into shit even though

we just wanted to hunt for women and drink Moet all day. Well this

day we went down to Q.B. where they were having a block party or

jam or something like they have on any Q.B. holiday. So the

atmosphere is good, music, bitches, and food. I got my man Peanut,

Devin and Dash with me. We were all mingling with everyone. All

of a sudden I see a Q-45 ride by. Little B informs me that is the guy who was shooting at Raymond and G-Man. Damn, Dash's birthday in the middle of a big BBQ block party, we got to get to work. I couldn't go home and let people know that we saw this guy, but gave him a full pass because it was Dash birthday. I sent Peanut to our hood to get the guns. The kid in the Q-45 parked down the block because the street was blocked off so he had to walk back to the block party. He must have got wind of who we were and tried to walk back to his car. I knew my man Rodu put the nigga onto us but there are no hard feelings bro. At this time we couldn't wait for Peanut to get back with the guns because he was either leaving or walking to his car to get his gun. Either way we had to move on him. He was a big guy so as we ran up to him he tried to turn and back us down but there was no doing that. Dash and I rushed him tackling him to the floor and Devin had a little knife and began poking this dude. As we were wearing him out Peanut got back and was pistol whipping him. The whole block party was yelling and screaming and just pissed off for us fucking this day up. We left this dude bleeding in the street, he wasn't moving. I was a little nervous until I got to my car and saw him up on one knee struggling to get up. "Fuck it, he's alive", I thought. Just as I said that G-Man flew by me on a motorcycle doing about forty towards this clown we just beat near to death. As the dude got to his feet G-Man drove up to him with a brick in his hand and as he passed him he smashed the brick on the dude's face doing forty miles an hour. The sight was painful to look at, the nigga hit the floor and I just knew he was dead. Shit! One month home and I'm in trouble again. The word was coming from the hospital that he was in a coma.

The police were in my projects immediately looking for me and G-Man. The people down there only knew a few Ravenswood dudes by name so they snitched on who they could. We went to the crib in Jamaica and laid low. After about four days I said, "Fuck it", I'm going outside to the hood. G-Man said he wasn't. I wanted to drive my truck as long as I could just in case I was gonna get knocked. It didn't matter. We had bail money and our block was clicking about five to ten thousand a day. See G-Man was the type to black out when it was time to pop, but be nervous when the boys were called. Hey, fuck it, nobody wants prison in their life. We ended up not being locked up for that shit and it was just hard for people in Q.B. to except that my little projects weren't going for the bullshit like they used to back in the days, way before I was repping. I never had issues about being bullied but older dudes in my projects at one time did because Q.B. had five times the amount of niggas that my hood had and guns weren't as available and most older guys down my way weren't home from jail at the same time. Well in the '90's things had changed drastically. Queensbridge dudes were still repping but my hood was also. May the best men win.

K.B came into my life; this guy was a character. Stand up dude but a goddamn mister know-it-all. The funny shit is that he and Dash are kind of smart. He was brought around by my man Chuck. Chuck always had a couple of dudes or weirdos he brought and tried to push them on us like the dude was a "real nigga". So he pushed this cat on us but he turned out to be all the way down. He got his shift and worked it and protected it like he was supposed to. Every shift had to have at least one gun on the block. Every shift had one or two lookouts depending on your shift and how hot it was. The morning shift which was 10AM to 4PM had one lookout and the 4am to 10am had one lookout. The other two shifts were prime time hours, crazy money but crazy hot. The only shift that was light on money was the 10am to 4pm. We would be happy to get between $1000 and $1500 them hours. $1500 was great, that wasn't too often. By this time every one of the bosses had nice cars and all the workers were happy getting paid and doing them after their shifts. We had lines of people wanting to join the team so no one was late or short on paper or did anything we didn't approve of, or they would get fired. Maybe beat up first, not paid, and then fired! All workers had to be on their P's and Q's or they would be replaced quickly.

Our workers didn't wear any bullshit gear. They went and brought Northface rain suits to hustle in for maybe six hundred. All types of Gore Tex boots, only shopping at Paragons and Tents and Trails. They were fly and everyone wanted to be a part of that. They had access to guns and bullet-proof vests. We let them manage money at young ages, it was perfect. At this point this was just our life, period. If someone got arrested, we'd bail them right out. They were never seeing Rikers Island unless they had to do a bid. They appreciated that. We took care of them so they were loyal. Not to say there was much of a choice. We would lay down the law something fierce on a disgruntled worker. I remember when K.B and Devin got knocked. The police watched from the roof and backdoors and caught a sale and walked to Devin's BMW and got drugs out the trunk. They also found the gun they had on the block. Recently Devin told me he was mad at me because I made everyone keep the guns on the block. Damn Devin! It's the drug game bro! His bail was 10 grand and we bailed him out and he went on the run. That put a strain on the situation because Devin, like me, was always on top of the business. Raymond and G-Man not so much. At one time it seemed like they only came around when the pack was finishing to get paid. As any good thing shit started to go bad.

Raymond and G-Man fell out which caused a major shoot out and the end result was Raymond decided to go on his own and set up shop on another side of the hood which everyone respected. After a while it seemed like I was taking care of everything. I can't complain too much because that's my nature but I still thought G-Man should come out more. Devin was even still around, working the nights so the police couldn't catch up to him. At one time Big D started coming back to Queens because shit wasn't going too well in the BX. I asked my dudes to put him down with us and they agreed. G-Man was really down with whatever I suggested, we hardly bumped heads when it came to business. Big D was out on the 10pm to 4am tour with my nigga Germ. He just had to supervise the block. This really wasn't his flow and he didn't like how many people were involved. What he didn't understand is that you have to change with time. Times change and things get done differently. After a short while he said he wasn't with it and went back to the BX. He used to come around now and then and get money from me and I had no problem doing for him. After a while it got old and when he asked for money I said, "Damn my nigga it seems you're extorting me." He laughed it off and left and I didn't see him for a long while.

One day I was at one of our cribs where we used to bag up work and was finishing chopping and counting and passing drugs to each worker. We gave each about 4 to 5 grand of drugs to hold at their house or someone designated to hold the drugs. When we did this people tried to get their shit and exit the apartment quick. So I got down to passing Dash his bag and he was with Nisha I believe. They walked out the door and I was heading right behind them.

There was one more dude in the house named Smitty. I called Smitty to come so we can leave together. He took too long so when I heard the back door slam I figured I would go catch up to Dash and Nisha. I closed the apartment door and walked down the hall. I got to the back door, I saw two people looking through the window in the hallway door staircase. I figured it was Dash and Nisha but when I walked out I saw two other people. Each playing a different wall in the staircase. Each had a gun in their hand. I looked up and it was Big D and one of his man from the BX Boobie. I grabbed Big D gun and tried to go down the staircase. He turned me and put me in the headlock from behind and put the gun to my head and covered my mouth, Boobie then came and put his gun to my stomach because I was still resisting. My whole life flashed in front of my eyes. They weren't even demanding anything so I thought it was just my life they wanted for me making that comment to him months before. They walked me back down the hall to the apartment, with my mouth still covered and one gun to my head and the other to my stomach. As we approached Smitty was coming out the house with a girl named Stephanie that we let live there because her Pops kicked her out of the house for hanging out with drug dealers. Damn Stephanie, this is what your Dad didn't want to happen.

They brought all three of us in the house and told us to go to the back room. Stephanie was scared to death and was crying but holding her composure the best she could. Smitty seemed calm at first, considering the circumstances. My mind was racing thinking how I could get out of this. They started asking for the drugs and guns. I told them everyone left with their shit. They ransacked the house and found five thousand in drugs in the house, plus Smitty 900 pay he had just got and about two guns. They weren't satisfied and put the gun to Stephanie's head and insisted she tell them where shit was. She let out screams of fear so I turned and told Boobie to leave her alone that they got what was in the house. He immediately turned and slapped me with the gun in the head and Big D told him, "Don't hit him again", Boobie then took all Stephanie's jewelry, the bullshit girls wear, rings and little chains. She was a young girl. They then told us to lay face down on the floor and cut off the light. Smitty went BONKERS and started yelling he didn't want to die. I told him to be quiet and lay down. We had one more trick left. It was that MAC 10 behind the door they never looked behind because they stood in the bedroom door. We all laid down and Boobie snatched my watch off my wrist. Big D again instructed him not to take my shit. I don't know but it seems like he didn't want me hurt, he just wanted the drugs and guns. It wasn't personal with me, he was sticking up our crew. Boobie then asked Big D should they tie us up which was stupid because there was no rope or wire to do so with, Big D said no. They made one more plea for the drugs and guns and said if they found anything else on their own they would kill us all. I then told them about the machine gun they would have seen if they closed the door. Boobie was hyped, "Oh shit, the Mac, the Mac," he said. They instructed us not to come out of the room as they backed out of the room and closed the door. Soon as I heard the front door close, I got up to console Stephanie. I then got up to check the house and told Smitty to come with me. He said, "Hell no, they said we better not move!" Crazy, let me be clear this was not my friend Boobie I was in jail with. This was a different slime ball named Boobie. This game was turning friends to enemies. Everyone wants their dollar, everyone wants to prove their point. Shit is dirty, but when should you back down, when should you back out? When is enough, enough? Well that little situation wasn't enough for me to quit. The problem was that at that time I still never had an end game. Never had that "NUMBER" amount that would make me say it's over.

Fuck it, we kept riding. I ended up buying a white ES 300. Shit was hard. There was a rule that when you bought a new car, you rode up the hill in Q.B. so everyone can get a look. The hill to us was like 125th or 145th street was to Harlem. The first time I came through, I had Biggie's "Who shot ya?" on Blast, I stopped and picked up my man Sherman. Known to the world as Sherm the WORM. A born damn terror. We laid back in my joint and rode around fronting all day. We had a lot of fun together and fucked a lot women together but this lil' nigga stayed in a lot of trouble. The winter came and I was having a big birthday party for myself. My birthday was like a national holiday. People expected me to have it with nothing but bottles of champagne and I always showed up and did one every year. Whether it was in a club, bar, crib, banquet hall or whatever, it was popping and had unlimited Moet and everything was free. This party was at my man Carl's spot. It was an afterhours spot, he rented it to me and it was quiet in the hood that day because everyone was preparing for my party. Everyone came though from all the projects and it was love. My man Shameek brought me a bottle of Moet almost the size of a midget. I had to drag the shit around the party all night and everyone was on their champagne high. Ice was known for his champagne campaign.

There was another party at Carl's spot that month also. It was for my home girl Shanel. Carl was her uncle and let her get the spot. The party was popping. Henny was flowing and vodka. I had champagne. I was with my home girl Big Tina and Dash and we were partying. All my home girls from Q.B. were there supporting Shanel. She also lived on 12th street so it was full of love at the spot. During the party my friend Tiny and my friend Elaine ended up bumping each other. Some drunk girl shit. It shouldn't have escalated but it did. I moved Tiny to the other side of the room and saw Elaine talking to her friend and staring at Tiny. I watched Elaine come across the party and punch Tiny in the face. The floor was slippery with drinks and Tiny slipped and grabbed onto me as she fell. I pushed Elaine and dudes weren't feeling that. Here it is again,

Ravenswood dudes violating. So a guy named Lord swung on me and we began to fight. A big brawl broke out that let out to the front of the club. Dash had the gun but was not sure whether to shoot these dudes or not, because he knew just yesterday I was cool with them and didn't want to go too far. Lord's friends noticed Dash had the gun and attacked him, disarming him. They passed the gun to Draws whom we've been feuding with, off and on for years. I could see shit was getting ugly. Me and Lord kept fighting. Draws ran up to the side of us and let me see he had the gun. I stopped fighting and stood there and asked him, "What's up?" He had red in his eyes and bust a shot to the ground. I figured he wouldn't shoot me because I saved his life at the Marc ballroom at a Mobb Deep show when we got into beef with Red Alert crew from BX and all of us from Queens had to stick together. They were beating him and smacking him with a bottle in the head and had him crawling. I got him up and out of the spot and Havoc but not before my wig was smacked with a Moet bottle. The brawl was intense. Draws and I were escorted to an ambulance where he thanked me for my help and my man Karate Joe was locked up for busting shots outside the club (him and Havoc), so I figured I had a card to play with Draws. Just then my man Dash came up and said something to Draws he then turned and shot Dash in the stomach. They both ran off, at the time I didn't know he was shot. Then my friend Nut started shooting in the air to break up the crowd and pushing me telling me to go home. In the process he ended up shooting one of his friends in the leg by accident.

Shots were popping everywhere, but Nut was trying to break shit up because he was a good friend of mine and of Lord and Draws. My car pulled up with Nisha driving and Dash in the passenger seat. I told her to get out of the driver's seat so I could drive. I was fuming about how shit had got out of control. I was upset that Lord was trying to front on me. While driving to my hood which was about two blocks away, Nisha informed me that Dash had been shot. He wasn't saying anything, I instantly turned the car and headed back to that corner. Lord and his crew were standing in front of the club. It looked like they were either arguing or discussing the situation. As I approached I sped and when I got to the corner where they were I jumped the curb and tried to run them niggas over. It was all in my eyes. They all jumped out of the way and one of them threw a bottle at my car. I turned the car and headed to my hood to load up. When I got to my block I had two flats from the move I pulled on the sidewalk. By this time I found out Dash was hit in the stomach and I shouldn't have done the reckless driving. I could have cost him his life. I told Nisha to take him to the hospital and when he got out of my car he threw up all over the place. I walked down the block to G-Man's house and called him out the window and he must have knew something because he came down with his gun and car keys. I told him what happened and he passed me the gun and we went down to Q.B.

We saw a group of dudes standing in front of the bar so we turned the lights off to his Maxima and I sat outside the passenger window and sped up to the group. They saw us approaching and was yelling, "Ice, chill!" I didn't respond with words. I responded Menace to Society-style, dumping shots and seeing dudes hitting the floor, crawling under cars and running. G-Man also was a great driver and spun the car onto the sidewalk so we could see if anyone was hiding behind cars that we can dump on. We emptied the gun and went home and got more guns. When we got back to Q.B., we walked up on Lord and his niggas disarming another dude that got into an issue with Lord's man Elliot at the party, pistol whipping the kid and knocking his teeth out. They might have shot him if G-Man and I didn't pull up because once we saw them we started shooting at them, and they did the same. There probably was 5 or 6 different gun battles that night leaving three people shot, one dude with no front teeth, and two people arrested. Lord ended up being locked up with a gun. The kid they fucked up pointed Lord out from the ambulance. Lord ended up doing 5 years for that night. All this jail time, all this shooting and the crazy thing is that Lord, Draws, Me, G-Man, Nut and everyone else involved got over all the situations and became great friends. Draws ended up getting killed over another situation that was just as stupid as the one I'm explaining to you, but that's how our life was. It seemed that God was sending me messages but I didn't see them. All this shit that I was doing and I was slipping through the cracks. Well in any game you eventually lose but my time hadn't expired yet. Things were rolling, beef was beef. Illmatic was the album popping and the streets cannot get enough of it. Nas had the GS Lexus, and I had the ES Lexus and we sometimes used to ride around the town back-to-back and front for the ladies.

I remember one day Nas, my man JP and I rode uptown to chill. I copped some Moet and we went and parked at St. Nicholas and 135th by the park. Once we got out and started sipping, it became like a zoo. Everyone wanted his autograph and/or to chill with him. I was seeing what the power of this rap music was doing. Even though I thought he had a great album, I was on the fence about who was better, him or Biggie. I also found a new artist that was coming out named Jay-Z. I saw a video he had made one day called 'My Lifetime.' I was living with my home girl Netfa and she used to tape videos. I came into the house and she was watching the video. It caught my attention which was odd because I didn't give too many rappers a shot. I mean, why would I? We had Mobb Deep, Nas, Tragedy Marley Marl, MC Shan, Cormega and a host of others in the neighborhood. This dude was different and the video was "HARD", I asked her who he was and she said some guy named Jay-Z. I kept my eye on him, I even went and bought the single. It was a black tape. At this time I was rolling thick with my friend Niecy. She was like a big sister to me and we clicked crazy. She had a lot of style, she liked mine too. We went everywhere together and she used to drive my cars in the neighborhood showing off. Everyone thought we were fucking but we weren't. In fact she wasn't fucking anyone in my crew. She introduced me to some of her friends from Jamaica that I got to roll with like Big John and Shebo. She fucked with them hard. They used to come to my hood with rented BMWs or trucks and we used to drink a ton of champagne. She also introduced me to her man named Knowledge. Him and I got cool and we would hang out from time to time. He was one of those "duel-boro" dudes. He was from Brooklyn and Jamaica. He was getting bread in and out of town. He had a white Four Runner and only drank Dom Perignon. We would ride in his car kicking it and drinking Dom P, I hated that he smoked cigarettes, I hated them period, but it was his car so I had to bear with it. He kept Niecy fresh and bought her a car, but she did things with me to make money on the side. She was smart, very street smart. I took her to clubs and treated her as if she was my girl. I spent whatever around her friends to make her look good and me look good. One day Knowledge came to me and told me he wanted to throw a big rap show in South Carolina where he was getting money or close by there. He said he was gonna get Biggie and Keith Murray to come and he wanted me to get Nas and Mobb Deep to come and he would pay them and pay for everything they needed. I wasn't making a dime off it but I said, "Fuck it I got you".

" It was easy to get the Mobb because I saw them damn near every day or someone from their crew. When I finally got up with Nas, he was with it and got paid half his money that day. Now understand this, the music was extraordinary back in those days but them guys weren't raking in the dough the way rappers in the 2000's were. I don't remember the numbers but the Mobb got a few thousands for the show and whatever they got, Nas got double. I held my part and Knowledge pulled out a few limos to my hood where I had the Mobb waiting to board to be taken where the tour bus would take people from. It was crazy; the Mobb brought all their infamous goon knuckleheads along with Tragedy and Capone from Capone-n-Noreaga. This is before CNN started but Capone wanted to be a rapper. Brooklyn dudes were deep, we were deep and on the bus each borough kept to themselves. Man, we brought so many bottles of Moet and Hennessy for my Queens niggas, it was crazy. I don't even think BK dudes thought we gave it up like that. I also had my man Shameek from Lefrak with me. Nas opted to drive his GS down to South Carolina to break the car in. I had no idea where Biggie or Keith Murray was. Knowledge assured me that they would be there. It really didn't matter to me because it was his show, my dudes were paid and we loved to travel to shows and fuck with bitches, go shopping and wild out. It was just plain old fun. We got to South Carolina and checked in to about 20 hotel rooms. Knowledge had no idea how reckless the Q.B. niggas could be.

My man Spunk also met us in South Carolina. He was getting money in North Carolina so he came to join us. Dudes tore this hotel apart, running up and down the halls fucking bitches, breaking shit, smoking weed etc. Me and Nas' man Grand Wizard ran into a fan of Nas that happened to be staying in the hotel. He wanted to meet Nas bad and had maybe two or three pounds of weed in his room. He was getting money but still was a slow country dude to us. I had Nas walk into the kid's room and introduce himself and spoke to the dude for a while and he must have passed Nas a quarter to half a pound of the weed. That was heaven for Q.B. niggas and they kept that nigga with us the whole weekend. This nigga was so open that he drove Keith Murray back home after the trip and moved to Q.B.

Nothing ever amazes me. Dudes are nuts. I remember the morning of the show going to a fucking arena to do sound check for the show. Nas was in awe and he told me he never done an arena that big before. I mean his album did just come out. The night of the show Biggie still hadn't arrived. It made them have to postpone the show to the next night which was a Saturday night. Knowledge and his people were heated and to make shit worse, the hotel where everyone was staying kicked us all out because of all the shit Mobb Deep young niggas were doing. So Knowledge now had to spring for rooms in another hotel. This shit wasn't going well far as profits up until now. They lost a ton of money for postponing the show, people started to think that none of the acts showed up. The next morning Knowledge got Biggie on the phone and let Nas speak to him. Biggie didn't think Nas was really there so he didn't come. Once he spoke to Nas him and Lil Cease flew to South Carolina ASAP.

I'll never forget when BIG walked in the room. I was open, he had his signature Coogi-sweater and shades with presidential Rolex. This day I think I was most proud of Shameek. Big was talking about his watch and how he bought it from I believe some rapper. It had diamonds but was a little scratched and not so clear diamonds. Shameek, who also had a Coogi-sweater pulled out his wrist and showed his presidential Rolex with diamond gleaming. Biggie was impressed, in fact impressed with the whole Queens shit. We outshined Brooklyn that day by a long shot! The show was a success, crowd was popping and even now that show would be one of the greatest of all time. The lineup was just crazy. Everyone was hot. We all shot to the after party where things got ugly. Hey, what did you expect? The infamous Mobb was performing then Capone and the south dudes got into it somewhere down the line. Capone was trying to talk to one of the southern nigga's girls. Hell no they weren't having that shit. Before you knew it, a fight broke out and it was the South against the North. A goddamn civil war. The Brooklyn/Queens separation was over, we all got it popping together. I thought a little then pulled Nas away from the bullshit. Cease and his other man, not sure who, got Biggie out of there. Next thing shots were fired. I mean, this club was shot to smithereens. I mean the framework of the club was destroyed. Everyone found their way to safety. The next day we all packed up and the bus came back. I rode with Nas, Jungle, Killer and Wiz back in the GS Lexus.

We had a ball on the way back. Niggas talk about that trip to this day. Niecy called me a few days later and told me them BK niggas respected our handle. I don't know why but for some reason them guys in Brooklyn used to think they are the only motherfuckers that got busy. Really strange to me.

So now I had gone to Freak-Nik down in ATL. At the end I had a big car accident in my Lexus racing to a party at Erick Sermon's house. His house was big and it sat on stilts and had his/her bathrooms that were cool. So I left the car there and sent money to my man Black Jayson that owned a store down there named Mr. Everything to get it fixed for me. Anyway after that I bought the Q-45. This shit was my shit, had a car phone and everything. A giant spaceship. As usual, I go up the hill and everyone is feeling my shit. My man Fat-Joe put the car in his name because even though he hustled he worked. I still had no license. Dash's birthday came again and again we were sipping and riding around and ended up in Q.B. A block party was happening and women were everywhere. We saw a group of girls and decided to pull up and holla a little. It was me, Dash, Peanut and G-Man. When

I pulled up and rolled down my passenger window to holla, we saw none other than Draws standing there talking to the bitches. It's like he saw a Deer in headlights. We had guns but I said chill and we pulled off. When I got about 20 feet away, Niecy pulled up on me. She was in a rental going the opposite direction from us. She was asking where we were going and what was up for the night and shit like that when I heard my back doors close. I looked back and Dash and Peanut were gone. I figured they were mingling with the girls at the block party while G-Man and I kicked it with Niecy. Not more than five minutes later, shots rang out and Niecy pulled off. I started to also but I remembered Peanut and Dash were gone. I saw them running into the block party shooting into the crowd chasing Draws. I had to wait until they got back to the car. There was chaos on the corner and I thought how stupid could they be to commit a shooting on the corner with all the children and older ladies out. I just knew this time we went too far. They jumped in and said, "Drive." I didn't, I started to curse them niggas out. Now we were hearing sirens and G-Man insisted that I drive off. We drove off past the police cars going to the scene. We got to my projects, parked the car in the lot and stood on the side of the building. Ten minutes later a police tow truck showed up and took my fucking car. Damn , bad fucking move. By the end of the night we found out that luckily only Draws was hit. We knew he wasn't telling but the women took my plates down and told the cops where we were from. About a week later Joe was able to get the car back from police. From that day on my car was hot I couldn't drive because I had no license, and they could arrest me for that now. I got in touch with my man Skins who went to college in West Virginia and could get me a West Virginia license quickly from a friend of his that was a state trooper, so I had to make a move down there.

I rode across the hill and came across Shanel. At the time we knew each other but weren't close yet. I asked her if she had a license and she said yes and I asked her to drive me to West VA to visit Skins who lived on her block so I could get mine. She agreed, how fucking wild is that? Out of the clear blue, she just went with me, the hood is really the hood as you can see. We took that long ride and had fun and got really close. Skins got his man to hook me up and we went back home. Skins eventually graduated from that college, then got knocked by the Feds for selling drugs on campus and sentenced to three years. Shanel became my right hand and started getting money with me. Her mom used to school me also but respected I was a young nigga getting it. I slept at her house, kept drugs and guns there. Everything really was love. My block was still clicking but me and G-Man's partnership was beginning to die out. I felt that we should split the block, still look out for each other, but I felt I was doing too much of the work while he sat back. In hindsight it was true but I did hog the work. I wanted to do everything. As Ellie said, "Kareem you're a tyrant." So we had a meeting to split up the block and split the crew. He was taking 12 hours and I would take 12 hours. He chose midnight to 12 in the afternoon. He left me the more hot hours for police but the most lucrative also. It didn't matter, I knew I was a natural born hustler. He took two workers as I did. All the workers wanted to come with me but it was business and we were all family. I was still clicking and buying new cars etc. and all was going well. Cormega came down on an appeal on his case, he caught the 5 to 15 on and we bailed him out for five grand. At the same time the 'sweet mafia' entered my life. The great Tee-Tee and her family of wild sisters. I love them girls and they started getting money with me also. These women brought a new type of fun to our block. The only thing was now it was not just work.

Everyone hanging out all night, everyone covering for the other if one is late or didn't show up. Switching work hours, what kind of shit is that? Fuck it I loved it too. We used to go to the Tunnel every Sunday now. Best club of the damn modern age. Big Kap then Flex. They rocked all rappers from our side's music, and we got crazy when we heard it. Bottles of Moet were only 65 bucks so we bought them by the caseload. Big was hot, Mobb Deep was hot, Jay-Z was getting hot, Busta was hot, it was crazy. Well Mega was home and looking for a deal. He was nice in rap but a little arrogant. Nas was the king of Q.B. as far as the streets were concerned. Shit, maybe even of all New York. I truly loved Nas music but constantly argued about if Jay-Z's album was as good, .He appealed to what I tried to do. See Nas' album was what I was doing and what most dudes in Q.B. we're doing. Smoking which I did not, drinking, having guns in the grass, shooting, pumping on the block etc. and he painted it so real because this was the reality of our neighborhood. The Nas Illmatic album had a 20th anniversary and a film made about it because it was so good.

Jay-Z on the other hand was rapping about the rewards of the game, going OT to hustle, whipping work, going to Vegas and reasoning why street dudes always made moves they made. I always said that Nas rhymed for the up and coming hustler and Jay-Z for the nigga that's a boss or at least trying to be. Jay Z rhymed about progression of the game while Nas' songs told you the dark TRUTH of the game. Like I said before, same painting, but seeing different pictures. They both spoke about the same game but from different points of view. This guy Jay Z was so ahead in thinking, that he dropped the same album ten years later and it still made perfect sense.

Anyway, I remember myself, Mega and Karate Joe had a meeting at Bad Boy through our man Biz who worked for Puffy. A lot of buzz was out for Mega because they knew he was from Q.B. and was Nas' man and he was getting out of prison. All of the makings of a star. I made sure my jewels were up to par and pulled up in a hot car and was fresh. Didn't want Diddy to think that Mega was desperate and would sign or fall for anything because you know Diddy will sign you to a wild deal that you'll regret later. So we came right to show Mega was strong. No demo or nothing, Diddy just let him spit in his office. Diddy seemed impressed and told Mega to make just three songs and come back. When we left I thought Mega was gonna be excited and run to do what he was asked. Instead he was a little standoffish and felt like Diddy said something wrong and refused to make the songs saying he will get signed without doing all that. Huh? I will give Mega this, he is adamant with the way he thinks. Well he was kind of right because Def Jam ended up signing him, they formed a super rap group called The Firm that had Nas, Mega, AZ and Foxy Brown. Foxy was my heart. I mean woman with hella sex appeal. She treated me like a king. I would do anything for her and her brothers and we became real close friends also. She would pull her buggy eye Benz up in my hood and pick me up or chill for a while. That's when I had my Tahoe. She wasn't scared to go to my hood and had a group of bad bitches who she hung out with. She was Def Jam's Queen. She didn't like people fucking with lil Kim. We would run into Kim some places and Foxy didn't want people associating with her people. I never met Kim so it was not a big deal but I knew Cease and Big from the time we did the South Carolina show back in the days. I toured with her and she used to let me perform on stage as hype man with her and Gavin (pretty boy). I fucking loved it, Mega was the only rapper that let me do that up until then. I knew a lot of big ones of that decade. She mentioned me in her 'ill-nana' album and I was in her video with Blackstreet 'Get-You-Home' that was big. Shit I did a lot of shit for the Mobb but they never mentioned me in their music. Yeah, I was in videos but never mentioned in songs. Even Nas mentioned me in his 'One Love' song then Mega mentioned me in his 'Reply Song'. Shit being mentioned was part of the gangster drug life to me. So thank you Foxy for pointing out a 'G' to the world when you didn't have to do it. For some reason Nas and Mega kept bumping heads on shit and their relationship soon got strained. I really don't know what happened that bad that it couldn't be fixed, but shit got really ugly. One day there was a big show at Madison Square Garden, I believe it was the Budweiser Superfest. Nas was on the card with Bone Thugs, Keith Sweat and some other acts. Instead of Cormega getting backstage passes he was handed nosebleed seats. He felt insulted as he should have, I mean he was part of The Firm. We made our way to backstage thugging shit out and when we got backstage Mega was flipping. Yelling at everyone telling them how he felt they shitted on him. He was getting heated and people were trying to calm him down. Steve Stout was having words with Mega and Mega was talking to Nas. Moose was Nas' bodyguard at the time and was trying to keep the peace. I said something to Nas or Moose and Stout went crazy. "Who the fuck are you?" he asked me, "Who the fuck is he?" he asked other people. They knew but he was about to find out, I threw some harsh words back at him, Moose intervened and grabbed me and asked me to chill.

Nas came to me and told me not to fuck his shit up which was not my intention from the beginning. Shit got calm but I walking past Steve Stout and he decided to say something to me, I instantly turned and busted his mouth open and tried to attack him when security got in the way. Mega was cool with it, in fact he was beefing with me against them as we were leaving. Everyone knew I was Mega's goon in the industry and he had no problem with it. It came back to haunt him. That night had been the last straw. Nas wasn't fucking with him anymore because he was loyal to Stout.. He kicked Mega out of The Firm crew and added another dude, Nature from Queensbridge. Once that happened everything went downhill. Def Jam put him on the back burner. He had a dope ass album that they didn't release. He had songs with Lil Wayne on the hook and songs with Carl Thomas and Mobb Deep and Foxy. There was a mix tape out with Nas, AZ and Nature with Mary J. Blige on the hook, and on the song Nature takes a shot at Mega talking about Mega being kicked out of The Firm. I heard it and called Mega and he said he wanted to flip on Nature. That evening I saw Nature while I was speaking with rapper Noyd. I called him over and asked him about the song. I don't even know what he said because my question was small talk and I ended up robbing him of his chain and giving him a chin check. I was loyal to my dudes.

I would pop whether they were there or not. I was getting plenty of money so I could have strayed away from the bullshit, but the streets had a hold on me. The competitiveness of rap in Q.B. became just as much as the drug game, I cut that story short because it was not worth too much of my time but shots were fired behind that and people ended up in jail. Even money was put on my head to the sum of 10K but dudes went to dudes who respected the goons not the rappers. I was insulted and told the same dudes I will give them twelve for one of them but he wanted the beef squashed. He fucked with all of us, this dude was my man, E Money Bags from Queens, R.I.P.

CNN started getting big in music and Capone and Nore was my brothers and still are to this day. These dudes fucked with me hard. We partied all the time, I used to look out for them if they didn't have money etc. Rap checks came in pieces so there was always times when a rapper didn't have money. I didn't mind because they got me in clubs for free, they showed love in the hood, we pushed each other's cars. At this time I think Capone and I had Denali Jeeps. Fuckin with them, I met the Murder Unit, goons from the Bronx. They took their name seriously and I will leave it at that. Shout out Deuce, Mike Booth, Six, Six-Seven and 00. I can remember hanging out with them and we had the time of our life. We use to party at Latin Quarters which they loved or Rhumbas in the Bronx. It was all love.

I wanted to throw a party in Winston Salem in North Carolina with Capone and Noreaga. I never asked for favors but this would be my first time. My man Fat Gary moved down there and had a friend who owned a club. The agreement was we get the door and the owner gets the bar. The name of the bar was Ice-House. Nore really got me upset on this situation because I was always good to him. Capone gave me no grief, he said he would come but wanted to bring a few people. I had no problem with that, I would give him that much because I wanted them to do the show for free. It was a favor so their man can come up. I rented a 18-passenger van and we drove with about five cars behind us. Nore kept giving me different things he wanted me to do. First he wants to bring five dudes, then he wants to fly, OK, then he wants me to fly all his people. Not OK. I am trying to make a dollar not fuck up money. Until the last minute, he played around so he ended up not coming. His protégé Mousilla and Maze, plus Royal Flush and Capone came. Cormega who was down in NC already getting money came also. We went deep and I got nice hotel rooms for all of them. They had a ball. Nore's people informed him that "Ice" was doing them right. We did radio down there promoting as if both of them were there. We went to the mall and they saw Capone and I knew the show was going to be a success. My brother-in-law was there and people thought he was David Hollister. Hey whatever was going to bring the crowd out.

The party went great and one by one all the artists performed. It was 20 dollars if you wanted to get in and 60 and 70 for VIP, which was just the back entrance. It gave you nothing extra. I made 18K and split it with Gary. That was a good weekend. Funny shit is, I told my man YG and he wanted me to do it again but he would get Mobb Deep. I was reluctant but I did it. Of course these dudes came a day late and Havoc didn't show up. They did no radio, no mall walk and the show was a flop. We made about 6 grand that had to be split three ways. YG was tight! hey that's the party promotion business. I was just living a good life and staying under the radar.

There was a big rap convention in Miami and Nas brought a lot of dudes from Q.B. down there with him. I flew on my own dollar with my cousin Shamel. I copped some Cristal and Dom P. We walked around South Beach all day. I was down there playing hard. Ocean, Super, Germ, Junior and some more dudes were with

Nas. Ocean also was dropping an album and was promoting that while he was there. One night I ran into them on Collins and it was Germ's birthday. They were going to get up with Nas but I told Germ he should roll with me and my cousin to a penthouse party. He did and I knew that was his best birthday ever. Clue and Fabulous was there and I got Germ pissy off champagne and battling Andre Rison that played for the Falcons in a rap. A lot of jokes and drinks, this was the life I loved. We got up with Nas the next night and went to Nelly's party. This nigga Nelly was rolling. He had maybe 30 dudes with him and he was sipping a magnum of Cristal and was sending cases at a time to his people. Meanwhile we were deep and only Nas and I had bottles. I brought some Dom and Nas brought some Cristal. We turned down an R-Kelly party and went for Nelly because he said he never met Nelly. That trip was light compared to one I would take later on in life.

Shotta and I started hanging out and we got close really fast. He would be with Nore so every time I was with Nore we would kick it. In 2001 things started to change, I think I had the Expedition and the Volvo S80. Not so sure but New Year's, new cars, that's how I moved. Now my mind is on automatic, I still don't have that magic number that would stop the ball from rolling so I am going with the flow. Going to the Poconos, Jamaica, Bahamas, Mexico, London, St.Marteen, St Barth's and Australia. My passport was filling up slowly but surely. My Rolex game was changing slowly also. As I am sitting here I am wondering how I should look at this life. I am sitting in the dayroom of Mod C-74 and reflecting on my life and probably wouldn't be doing it if the hammer wasn't dropped on me. Anyway, now I am on this prison ride and it seems I don't have a care in this world. All this shit seemed like it needed to happen to me. It's pouring out like an open faucet. It's cleaning me, it's freeing my mind. I hope by the end of this harmless confession that I get some type of closure to some of my thoughts. I am here trying to avoid some guys who may influence me to commit some more crime or even worse crimes. I mean, I read self-help books, I read finance books. Everyone in here has a story to tell and I wonder if theirs is true? How much of it is true? I wonder why they are not preparing their mind for when they get home. Why aren't they planning ahead. I try to drop a jewel every now and then to see if anyone bites but very few do. I see why people say they don't want to ever come back, but if you are here why bullshit around? I lived a full life and I am only up to the beginning of the 2000's. I have another 13 years to go before I get knocked off by snitches and wire-tapped phones and video surveillance. My neck is stiff from writing and my hands numb but I am in a zone of releasing all my pain and highs and lows on this paper. In here I get a chance to exhale. After about a twenty year run, I finally get a chance to put my head up above the water and take a deep breath. I mean I am about to watch the World Series' and I think to when I was at game six at Yankee stadium the night they won their last world series with Derek Jeter on the team. I was there, me, Rock and Rah, we paid some scalpers $1400 and got neck passes to get in. I think about so many things that make me smile while I lay in my bed at night in this cube.

Well as I said 2001 things changed for me. One night we went to a new club that just opened and I was there with my friends from the hood. I ended up leaving the club and left my car with Raymond. They all ended up in some altercation that night where they cut some kid up, beat some dude and some girl got shot. All this was going on and they were riding around in my car so people assumed I was there. Where I stayed that night had poor reception. I was deep in Long Island, Wheatly Heights. So the next day when I got some reception I found out what happened and went to get my truck. The shit was covered in blood in the inside. These dudes couldn't even clean the damn car out! Anyway the police were looking for a few of them and even me. I knew the people who got hurt so I went to the hospital to let them know the deal. They were surprised to see me because they knew they already snitched on me. I got that straight quick but they said they only said my name because it was my car. Well I told them the same way they got it wrong for me, is how the whole thing was a big misunderstanding. They weren't going for it. If the guy that got beaten up was the only victim, I could have got them to fall back, but they showed me the dude that got hurt. His face was really torn up, and then they had the nerve to add insult to injury, they picked up and just shot a bitch in the stomach. Both of them were in the hospital. I had my work cut out for me. Of course, money was involved. My man Peanut got caught first. He was drunk that night and had to hustle his shift in the morning. He fell asleep on the bench and woke up to police with the blood from the guy on him and cracks in his hand. Then my man

Chuck got picked up. I was able to get them to drop the charges on Raymond and Forever before they got knocked. They had to pay, I believe. Four grand. My man Banano was also on the case. Long story short, that happened in '99 but after everything was over Chuck got time served. Banano got something light but Peanut ended up getting 12 years. Fast forward…….

Now I was in the World's Famous Pub in Q.B. which is a hangout spot for me on the weekends. I love the owner and he loves me. I was with Niecy, my man Banano, K.B. and Forever. When I got there, I saw an unfamiliar face down there but he was sitting at the table in front of us having drinks. I was having drinks and waiting to get picked up so I can slide off to my crib in Fresh Meadows. Niecy wanted to hold my car but I told her she had to wait until my ride got there because my gun was in the car. She said cool so we just drank as we waited. So the fucking guy that got beat up was in the bar and he was drunk and he wanted to keep talking to my man Banano about the incident saying how he didn't want to snitch or didn't snitch or some bullshit. Banano did time for the case so he didn't want to talk about the shit. This dude insisted to keep talking about it. So Banano went outside with him to talk, K.B. went also. They took the kid across the street and began to fuck that nigga up. Now he got his ass beat up since he would not shut up . I saw the commotion from the window and Niecy and Forever and I went outside. We did not approach the fight though, I was waiting on my ride. The mysterious dude also came outside but he went across the street, walked into the block and came back out and walked to the dude that got jumped. By now, Banano and K.B. were on the side of the street where I was and not paying much attention. I saw the mystery guy give the other kid a gun, but the kid gave it back. I figured that the kid was upset so I should go talk to him , I know him not the mysterious guy. I first came across the street saying, "Don't shoot! No shooting here!" At this time, Niecy had gone and my ride had come. I could have just left but I wanted to handle the situation first before someone got hurt. I went across the street to talk to the victim with Forever behind me. My man Skins also came across the street. I didn't want Banano to come because it would probably make things worse. I thought that him and K.B. were still around but later on they would claim that they had already walked off. Anyway, I approached the kid talking to him but I really had my eyes on the guy I didn't know, because I saw he had a gun. I acted like I was walking towards the guy I know but turned and grabbed the mysterious man. He was in shock. I grabbed his shoulder and waist to disarm the dude. He started to pull away so I slammed him to the ground. He held on to me so I fell down on top of him. I managed to get the gun off his waist but it was on the ground. I leveraged my body to where he could not grab it but I wasn't able to either. I was able to slide it to the side and my man Skins picked it up. The dude and I both jumped up then I heard two shots. I looked at Skins, he was pointing the gun at the kid then I looked at the kid he was pointing a gun at me. I didn't know that the kid had another gun on him. He brought one for his man and I took it for granted that it was the only one he had. I wasn't sure who let the two shots off. Then I stepped back and saw blood on my shirt. I got shot. I said, "Forever, hold up son. I think I got shot." I pulled up my shirt and sure enough I was hit point blank range with a big old .45 automatic. When reality checked back in for everyone, Forever grabbed me and turned me to run, which maybe I should not have done. When people run, it gives others power. As soon as I turned and ran he started dumping crazy. The next shot broke my leg and I fell and I was dead weight. I felt another hit my leg, one through my boots into my toe. When the shooting stopped I looked up and he was damn near standing over me but ran out of shots. No shots were fired from the gun that I took from him.

I ended up being shot five times and almost had to get my leg amputated. There was one strong blood vessel left in my leg and if it could not pump enough blood along my leg it would have to be cut off. Either that or I die. My sister did not want to make that decision. When I woke up she told me how lucky I was to still have a leg, let alone that I did not die from the point blank shot in the stomach. That's one of the times I was happy that I had a little fat on my body. I had to get a few surgeries and had pins in my leg for six months and was in a wheelchair for the same amount of time. The first week I was in the hospital 3 niggas down in Q.B. got shot, behind me getting shot. My niggas wouldn't let up. Anyone that fucked with the kid, helped him lie low, armed him or anything was going to get it. Homicide was coming to the hospital to threaten me about stopping the shooting but they didn't seem to care about my condition. So fuck them! I was trying to run my business from the hospital but it was hard because at this point I had some young dumb niggas pumping. I had moved to the other side of my projects because where I was at before got absolutely too hot, like Biggie said that all the money I stack had to use it on bail. A lot of little beefs were going on and it would not slow down till I got home. By the time winter came around, I was walking again. People thought my leg wasn't strong because how it looked but it was probably stronger than before but I let them believe it was weak.

Skins, now that's a good friend. When the shots went off and people saw that he picked up the gun that I knocked away from the dude and he didn't fire, people were screaming. They didn't believe the gun was jammed or broken or whatever because why would the nigga bring out two guns and one is broken? I didn't have an opinion. I just had the word of a good friend of mine that insisted the gun did not work. It was a situation where everyone had to think fast and maybe he did freeze but maybe not. Either way, I was not upset with him. People thought I gave him a pass because I thought he was a college dude that was not in the street or whatever. They were wrong. Although he did go to college and graduated with a

Bachelor's Degree from a college in West Virginia on a basketball scholarship, I did look at him as a street dude. We all grew up in the streets and he had already done a Fed Bid for hustling at his college. He went to prison right after he graduated. The reason I was not upset is because this situation came out of nowhere. I was waiting for a woman and I was slipping, no beef was in the air. So when or if he didn't react the way I did or the way people said he should have even though they were not on the scene to understand, I didn't care. Half the people talking didn't ride with me after the shooting anyway, so their opinions didn't matter. As my team was popping niggas day-to-day, the guys with so much to say played the background and rolled into the hospital time to time to tell me someone else was shot. That never went into my head. Now if we made a conscious decision that night that we were going to Q.B. gripped up and it was a situation where we were looking for trouble or just mobbing up then, I would have expected the gun to work, etc. I would have been upset and maybe not fuck with him, but never snake him. I loved him and him me. That nigga sat in the hospital with me every day that summer. I couldn't get rid of him. I know he felt bad that I got shot. I told him numerous times to go enjoy the summer, but he'd rather sit by my side. He might not have been as aggressive as others I grew up with, but if I told him to do something with me he rolled, whether it was about bread or violence. He and I almost blew the wrong person's head off one day. We laid on the roof one morning, waiting for an enemy of ours. Thinking we spotted him, we ran down on the guy pulling our pistols. When we got close to the guy, it was the wrong person that was scared out of his fucking mind, and with a good reason to be. We broke out and when we got back to where we stashed my car, can you believe someone had broken in and stolen my damn radio? Crazy! Maybe his balls are not the biggest but he has some. Besides that, I know he will never stab me in the back under no circumstances. Thanks for your friendship Skins.

The chase for the shooter kept up. My leg was permanently changed. To think the leg almost had to come off. A few months later we got word that the kid was around Q.B. and hanging out on his block. I was not healthy yet, still sitting in a wheelchair. The wolves went into action though. It was an early sunny afternoon in the summertime. K.B., Dash and Forever crept down to his block.

The only problem was that no one really knew what the kid looked like. He was a nobody until he pulled his unspeakable crime off. After that, he was a folk hero to a certain extent. Some people were happy that he almost destroyed the "evil" Kareem AKA ICE and some people just rooted for him because he was from Q.B. He even began to pull stick-ups. At the local gambling spot in the neighborhood even once claiming he did it because the owner was cool with me. Well, this day. It was a search and destroy mission for his ass. When they entered the block, it was crowded so they really were trying to figure out who he could be. People on the block knew this was war so when they spotted my team, they began to grab their children and run for cover. It started a small frenzy. In the midst of it all, the chump stood up to see what was going on, and he caught eyes with the shooters. Instantly, gunfire erupted. Everyone had a .45 caliber or better, especially since that was the weapon I was shot with. He returned fire as he ran. They gave a minor chase then he dropped. They figured that mission was accomplished. They turned to run back to the getaway car where they parked on Vernon Blvd., a straight way back to our project. The only problem was, Forever didn't run back to the car the way it was planned. He instead kept running through Q.B. and took another way home. So K.B. and Dash were sitting in the car with two hot pistols and no car keys. Hey! You can't make this shit up! At this point sirens are all around and they needed to make a move. They left the guns in the car and went into the River Park, which is also on Vernon Blvd. and hid there until it was safe to leave.

The housing workers that cleaned the buildings in Q.B. saw them get into the car and saw them get out and leave and informed the police. The police took their car and found the guns in the car in addition to a read out beeper, the two way pager that people had back in the days. There were messages on it that linked K.B. to the shooting. He was subsequently arrested for the shooting and guns along with another case and ended up getting five years in prison. To make matters worse, the Chump they had come to get had a bulletproof vest on and survived the incident. Some say he got hit up and the vest saved him, while others say he dropped to throw the dudes off. Either way we were not going to let it rest. It was war times. I missed catching this clown by split seconds. I would go to Q.B. and hang in the local spots where I knew he would or should come if he knew I was on deck, but the coward never came. Many dudes that were supposed to be cool fed him info as to where I was and/or who I was with but I figured in a matter of time the showdown would come. I would be doing a life sentence or death or with my luck, dodge another bullet. At one point, I even had to holla at Nas because this little nigga was from his block and I heard his brother Jungle had the dude lying low with them on tour. Nas and I discussed this issue and resolved it. That kid was Jungle's friend but Nas had no foul intentions to want to help the kid. At this time my man Charlie Saruti had a bar that was off the hook in Woodside projects. On the weekends, everyone attended. I knew sooner or later I could catch the kid there. Charlie always let me know who was at that spot before I came and always let me in with the pistol. I loved him for that. He was good friend to me. One night, the kid came and he came with Nas' brother, Jungle. I got the word and by the time I got my shit together and got there, they had left. One reason was because Charlie did not let them in with pistols. The stress of this situation went on for what seemed to be like years to where the issue was discussed with my family about me doing time over this. No matter what, I always think ahead, you heard?

Anyway, one day there was a bus trip to Atlantic City. It was the same weekend as Funkmaster Flex's Car show. Floyd Mayweather was fighting out there that weekend and my man Skip had run into some tickets and gave them to me. So I called my cousin Nickels and went down to A.C. with him. He was going anyway because he rapped and wanted to promote his mix-tape down there. He and I tried to hang but he's just difficult to deal with. He drove his X-Five BMW and I drove my car. Not sure which kind of Benz I had at the time. Things were cool at first. Even when I called his brother Looch on the phone and let him know things were smooth, he could not believe it and insisted it would not last. It did not.

We got down there early so we had time to go to dinner and I also informed him that the kid that shot me might be on the bus and if he was, I was going to pop on him. Nickels was uneasy with that for whatever reason but he informed me that he had the pistol in his car. I think he said that to see if I was bluffing. Later, when the Q.B. bus got out there, we hung out with a few girls I know at the Trump Beach bar. I think this is the night I first met my home girl Crystal.

Anyway, in the middle of drinks I told Nickels I might need the pistol in his car and he got irritated with me and I was fucking his mood up. I left that issue alone. Since Nickels and I went down to A.C. last minute, there was no room available but a white dude at the beach bar was able to get us one for $500 for the night. He was feeling us and we bought him a few drinks. Nickels was reluctant but I figured damn, I am taking him to the fight and if we split the room, it is $250 a piece. Damn nigga. Things were starting to unravel between us. I tried to be as patient as I could. Anyway, we got the room. My man Big Rah, Shameek, Shapel and Judah from Lefrak was down in A.C. and gambling hard. I went to the craps table for a while and Nickels went to the slots saying that he didn't feel the vibe. Big Rah went with Nickels because they were cool and fucked with two girls who were sisters. After the fight, which Mayweather won of course, and the drinking and gambling, I ended up with Nickels late that night or I should say early morning. I was chilling with two girls from my neighborhood in our room. He came in looking crazy but did not say anything. He told me that he had just lost $500 to the slots. I said, "Damn cuz", then said my man Judah lost eight grand to craps. The statement took this dude into an uproar, "I don't give a fuck about your man, fuck him." Yada yada yada, so on and so forth. I was thinking, this dude is mad because the girls are here and I said someone lost more money than him gambling? Well, it was true. I didn't upstage or grandstand on him because I didn't say that I, myself lost shit. We ended up having an argument to the point where I tried to give him his $250 bucks that he put to the room just so he would leave. Fuck outta here! He refused at first but later picked the money up before leaving a few hours later. Typical Nickels.

My phone reception was poor down there and I had missed a lot of calls. When I saw how many I had missed, I started to return the calls. Everyone wanted to know where I was and if everything was OK etc. I told them I was in A.C. and everything was cool. That's when I was told that the kid that had shot me got murdered on his block that night and the dude that killed him got murdered while leaving the scene trying to get back to his car. I was shocked and a little relieved also, but wanted to know who killed the shooter and why. I came to realize that the shooter was a victim of this fool's gambling spot robbery. He robbed gambling spots in Q.B. a couple of times and this guy was there once and was not going to tolerate that. He was not from Q.B.; he was from Jamaica Southside. May that man rest in peace. Shit I would have helped pay for his funeral. This is where people would say things happen for a reason. Yeah. But it had nothing to do with me. He was killed for an act he did to someone else. This wasn't a blessing from God to me. God let us live our lives out and judges us for our actions after we die. He does not interfere in day-to-day activities. That's what faith is about. If you knew that God would do this or that and you knew that in the end everything would be good if you just follow him, then everyone would just do the right thing and wait for the afterlife. Faith is what you have when there is no proof that you will get anything for your actions. I believe in God and know I will be judged for my actions and I know I have to set things right with God before I die or I won't be in a good place.

So, what kind of a woman is built for my liking? I want the woman that's the prettiest and the purest out of the bunch that has goals. A focused woman that doesn't say what she thinks she's expected to say but what is in her heart. A sexy woman. One that cares to some degree of what others think of her. She wants to rise to the occasion of popularity through her fashion statements. A driven woman that knows when to slow it down and let her man take the lead. To know how to sway his opinion when she disagrees without seemingly going against him. A woman that caters to my likes and wants. One who finds out what those likes and wants are on her own. A woman that can live the same way very rich, that she can live poor. Strong is sexy to me. Not physically strong, but mentally strong. Sensual is sexy to me. Being thoughtful and witty is sexy to me. I don't know if this is too much to ask for but if I could get all these in a woman, it would be ideal. I guess all the women in my life had at least one of those qualities in them.

If they were hustling with me, I loved their street savvy. I loved their courage. Most women who are ready to hustle are riders. They have your back to the end. The ones I dealt with certainly did. I always tried to make them want the most out of hustling. Buying cribs, cars, jewelry or whatever they wanted. I spoke to them and treated them a little nicer than I did the fellas. They were kind of spoiled. If the fellas were cold, I wouldn't hear of them leaving early before their shift ended or standing in the buildings out of sight for the customers to see. The women could do both. In those ways, I wasn't fair but when it came to the count and to the money, they got the same scolding the guys would get if shit wasn't right. I was big on protecting our women. I am like that with any woman I am fond of. I am just old school like that I guess. I remember one time I came on the block and there was some type of a confrontation with the police and my girl Tee Tee. The police ran down on her and she resisted and ended up hurting her leg before she was arrested. As I was being told the story, I was getting furious because we had look-outs plus management watching over her. No one else was arrested. I was thinking how the hell they could let the police beat her up and arrest her. I didn't care what happened or how many police were there, if she fights then they all fight. I gave all the guys on deck a good tongue lashing that day. I bailed her out and heard her side of the story. As I figured, dudes just didn't want to get arrested. That same week, I was arrested for assaulting a police officer. Yeah, the same cops always came and thought they could harass or intimidate us, but they knew that on any given day, I would start a fight. In my mind, I always thought that even the police just want an easy day.

Nobody wants to be tussling on the floor every day. The police threw her around and I felt I had to throw one of them around. Sure I was arrested, but he was gone. It was like the bully that the guy he tries to bully doesn't back down. Eventually, the bully bothers someone else. So sometimes the police come out and I see they were ready to rumble and I would back the troops down but I know they are not ready to rumble all the time so I picked my battles. Street warfare, that's all it was. I was protecting me and my own. When you protect them, they will protect you. Tee-Tee jumped into fights that I was having so much I started feeling like I was the girl. I was good to all the girls. They got their paychecks but I'd still take them to clubs or buy them clothes or boots. That was like a magnet for other women to want to be around. Either to hangout or to work for this gracious, giving and thoughtful boss. Sometimes I even left them with my car when I went on vacation. Now Shanel was the woman that worked for me, but was my damn boss, very demanding. Her pay was her pay, then I would have to buy her $600 DKNY coats or $300 Gore-tex boots. Back then, we stayed in Paragon Sporting store. I didn't mind. I loved all the girls I dealt with in one way or the other. They gave me their loyalty as well as their hearts and some their bodies. Yeah, in the mid-nineties, casual sex was just the wave. Get high or drunk, fuck then back to business without blinking an eye. The women probably wanted more casual sex from the guys than we wanted from them.

Maxi got knocked off by the D's trying to grab a cup of champagne out of my hand while I was driving to a friend's funeral. Police pulled us and searched her extra hard, thinking she took drugs from me but it was just the cup in case they tried to say I was drinking and driving. They did find drugs on her and arrested her and tried to get her to say that's what I passed her. She stood tall. They took my car apart trying to look for more shit, but found nothing. She was arrested and bailed out pronto! The police were so thirsty for an arrest that they overlooked a pistol I had under the rug. So instead of a weapon collar, they had to settle for a small simple possession. This is my rider. She entered my life in 2001 and has been around ever since. She was on the streets but I guess dudes did not see her potential until she got with me. Yeah, I groom people and wipe the dust off of them so they can see who they really are. Yeah, people probably have stories about her from her young days, but when she grew up them same dudes could not get a piece of her. Dudes love this girl. Sometimes I think guys loved her so much because they thought she was my girl and they wanted to have something on me. Thing is she wasn't my girl, she was just loyal to a dude that did not sell her a dream. Whatever I said I would do to get her right, I would do. I did not use her. I explained every step of the way, the situations that we were in at all times. I allowed her to eat. She was fly and stylish and knew how to handle men. Dudes used to address her and tried to get her to their camp. Ha ha! How foolish was that? Most of the people knew her before I did, so why wait until after she is with me to want her? I never pressured her to never fuck with others because I knew that my situations were the best anyone that our neighborhood could offer. But she talked a little too much, much too much but her good outweighed the bad. More importantly than that, she knew who she was, never denied her past but wouldn't make the same mistakes again. Why? Because she got with some real niggas with love for the people that we had on board with us. I know that she would burn in the fire for me. Her loyalty has been tested and she has passed. It was never tested by making things up because that's not how I work. I wait for the card to play then see how people give it up. She is one of the rare street hustler girls from Long Island City. She runs in the ranks of Shanel, Tee-Tee, Nisha and Niecy, even though Niecy never sold a drug since I knew her but she was very involved with my life at a point and time.

Then there was Donna and Keisha none of these women folded under pressure of police. I'll never turn my back on any of those women. Any success that I have, they will always be part of it. These people are part of my journey and will never be forgotten.

In 2002, I got shot again. This time by my old friend. I was going through some serious shit at the time so I really never could respect the timing of the shooting. If we had a problem that serious, there was plenty of other times he could have handled it and that's all I will say on the subject. So I will tell you that the game is vicious, love changes and best friends become strangers. Through all, this vicious life I lived, I never crossed my man. I never tried to stick a knife into a friend's back. Shit! I felt bad when robbing people I was not OK with. A nigga can sleep well around me if we're cool and a nigga can depend on me if we are cool.

At this time, I am rolling with Shotta and my Chinese man. Shotta went to prison for a few years and the Chinese guy and I had formed a great friendship with respect for each other. We made a lot of money together. He kept producing even when it was a drought. I remember when I first met him from my man Los and Los told me that he was paid, which I did not believe. He had the old Maxima and my nigga Los exaggerated a lot. He was good hustler and knew a lot of people. Product was good quality and I could also get the arm (consignment) if I needed it. His prices were higher than most but he was straight business so I fucked with him almost exclusively. After a while, we were pulling up on each other with new cars on a regular basis. Different Benz's, etc. He was big on Henny, when I first met him, and you know I will drink it but Moet is my drink. This dude got his hands on everything but everything was at a high price. I did not know whether he was getting ripped off or just ripping me off, but money was being made. I became known for having high prices because I had to sell them high because this dude sold them to me high. But I was also known for best quality, most dependable and being a no nonsense businessman.

The Rolex game was changing a little. Now I might have had two at a time or three instead of just one. He was big on watches. At one time, he had 12 Rolexes and his girl had one. He was the type to read the Robb Report and really buy shit out of there not just go window shopping. He was younger than me by two years. He trusted me and I trusted him, bringing his family to my family Christmas parties and Thanksgiving dinners. So when our mutual friend Shotta was coming from jail, we decided to throw a bash. It was shocking that on the night that was supposed to be a celebration also brought tragedy at the exact same time. I found a place where I would throw the party for my bro Shotta. It would be at a bar/restaurant in Long Island City. That's not too far from the big Citibank building. I knew the owners and they let me get the spot. Our whole crew brought a lot of champagne and invited everyone we knew from Brooklyn to Lefrak to Long Island City. We had my "peeps" as they would say from Fort Greene Carlton Avenue side. The ones that were not in the Feds because there was a big sweep out there due to a violent outbreak on the NYPD for killing one of the best people from Brooklyn I've ever met. My great friend, FLY TYE. He was related to the infamous Supreme Magnetic. I hung out there for about half a year straight every day while I was lying low. I was being investigated. I loved it out there. They were good people that enjoyed each other's company and had each other's back. Shout out to the "peeps": Live, Keisha, Snoop, etc. Of course, we had the whole Lefrak City from which is where Shotta was from. My lil man who grew up and went out of town and blew up, brought plenty of Rose and Ace of Spade to show Shotta he had made it because he was not getting paper before Shotta left. He also went and bought a mink with my man Banano. I saw them when I pulled up in the parking lot in my hood. There I was going to count out the bottles of Ace of Spade, Dom P and Rose I had already brought. They were sharp. I knew my man Rah was eating so I wasn't surprised with his amount of bottles but Banano! I was in awe and confused. This was the cheapest man on the planet. He hustled, but not to have extra money to buy that type of coat and a case of ACE also? This nigga owed me bread as he stood in front of me at that moment come to find out he also put a $1000 toward Rah's coat and told him don't sweat the money. He told me that he caught a good robbery and did not have to use a gun. He was the type that always looked for an easy robbery, if he could but would use the gun to do it also. When it came to good old fashioned pumping crack he hated it, but he did it because he had to earn day-to-day. I always had to front him work. In these years, there was no locking the block down, everyone did what they want in the hood I just supply the work if they had the money. My close friends always wanted their work fronted to them. He told me he had been working a fiend that had a lot of money for about a month and it finally paid off. He told the fiend that if he gave him 20k out of his account he would be partners with him and he would never have to buy crack anymore because he was his partner and he would also kick him back a few grand weekly. Foolish fiend! It worked, he passed Banano 20k and Banano had plans to buy a BMW that he'd seen on the used car lot in a few days. Tonight though, he was spending with the crew.

Banano was famous around our way for an infamous robbery he pulled in the big park in the projects that we call the DS Park. That is where he robbed Lamar Odom. Yeah, Lamar Odom when he was playing with the Lakers. Lamar was cool with dudes in my hood so he would visit the neighborhood a lot. In my eyes the robbery should never have happened. He was Butch's homeboy and he came through. He had been coming around since he was 10 years old playing in tournaments. Somewhere there was a miscommunication, as to if Butch was being taken care of by Lamar. He wasn't but the night shit happened, Butch said Lamar would look out for him that night. Banano was informed that Butch did not want anything to happen to Lamar but Banano thought Butch was lying about Lamar looking out for him and decided he was going to get him anyway. No one was aware of Banano's intentions since he was told everything was cool. When Lamar was leaving and about to take a dude to a club, I heard a shot go off. When I turned around I saw Lamar against the gate with Banano in front of him pointing the gun at him telling him to take his watch off. Lamar had a twofaced diamond Jacob watch. You flip the face and it had a different face with different diamonds. The shit was bananas. Lamar pleaded, saying, "Yo man. It's me LO." It was too late. It had to happen. I thought about intervening but the robbery began and I was not going to fight a nigga that put holes in people for me before, just to save a multimillionaire that's really was not going to break Butch off that night anyway. Banano took the watch and about seven grand that he had in the pocket and broke out. For the record, I loved Banano and would have died with him but did not agree with the move. Like I said people see shit different from me. I had always been proud that celebrities could and did hang in my neighborhood and felt comfortable coming. They're supposed to be safe within our hood with us. That robbery changed that. I had a lot of celebrities come check me from Nas, AZ, Foxy, Mobb Depp, Kurupt etc. They all came heavy and was able to be relaxed as hell. Lamar should have been the same because Butch is a true "G" from Ravenswood and put a lot of money in dudes' pockets over the years.

Anyway, back to the night of the party. Banano and Big Rah were ready to party and so was I. My home girls came from Virginia to show love, Q.B., Ravenswood, everywhere. Nobody misses an ICE party. They didn't give a fuck if they knew who Shotta was or not. The party was popping and we all was taking flicks. There was a light car Show outside because we all had whips. I think I had the R500 Benz at that time. I had that the next year then it was. It's crazy. I started out buying cars that were two years old. Like I said if it was '92 I would have a '90 now it switched to. If it was '90 I would have a '91. "My game has grown prefer they call me William

"I went from Levi to guess to Versace now it's diamonds like Liberace." Do you get it? Of course the dudes from AQ came but they were not invited and they got into something with others who were invited. The crazy shit is that the Q.B. kids that were invited asked if they bring could their guns in case they got into something when they leave the party with the dudes from AQ. I'm not sure who gave the OK but it was given and not by me. Anyway the dudes from Astoria ended up getting escorted out of the party. So the party seemed to be a success and it started to wind down. Everybody was pretty drunk and of course a fight broke out with two unlikely characters. My friend Rick and my great friend Yon, Yon is from QB so when the boys from QB saw him fighting, their natural reaction was to help Him. They were not familiar with Rick since he was not around often in Queensbridge and did not grow up in our neighborhood. The fight went from inside and spilled out onto the street. Yon and Rick knew each other so we were going to just let them get shit off of their chest and let that be that, plus I was tired and drunk from the party and was not in the mood to be breaking shit up. When the young Q.B. dudes got involved, I had to intervene, trying to tell them to mind their business and that Yon and Rick knew each other. Yon didn't deal with these young boys anyway. They were not peers.

Anyway a commotion broke out. The commotion was crazy and a few guys were getting pushed to the ground. I tried to stop them because I really did not want shit to escalate too much. The shooter was standing right next to me. I looked at him and his gun was raised in the air. He was trying to break the commotion up, but that was a bad idea. I looked in his face and he was in shock then I heard someone say "Joe is dead". I instantly started looking for Joe. Then I looked to where the shooter was looking in shock and saw my man Banano laying on his back with a hole at the center of his head with white puss oozing out. I turned back and the shooter was running off, Raymond gave chase. I was stuck and could not believe this had happened. I went into the bar and got my gun as my blood was boiling over. I told Yon to meet me in my project parking lot. I drove there and parked my car, got in his and told him to drive me to his hood. I was trying to cut those little motherfuckers off. Yon and I circled the hood a few times and there was no sign of them. I decided it had to be gunplay so I told Yon to wait and walked to one of the blocks I saw one of the kids coming out of the building with two dudes. I opened fire on them. One pulled a gun and returned fire as they ran off. By this time, the sun was rising and Yon drove me back to my hood and the beef was on. It was determined rather quickly that there had to be bloodshed. That Monday, most mothers kept their kids home from school. Both of the neighborhoods were on the edge. Everyone knew that the shooting was an accident, but it was hard to digest. Banano's funeral was in a church in QB. Damn, do we make shit hard for ourselves or not?? They had snipers on the roofs of the projects and barricades to direct traffic and every damn police car in the world. It looked like they were going to make sure that nothing happened. Nothing happened and the shooter never came back around and ended up getting killed in Brooklyn at a basketball game months later. The hood is funny because both the victim and the shooter were from different hoods that fucked with each other but the street could not respect a ending anything less than death or prison. Why the fuck do we want to stay in this lifestyle when 80% of the niggas in the street will never flourish in this life? RIP Banano! RIP Darren. We've got to keep pushing on though that it is hard.

I started fucking with a young dude from Q.B. named Manolo. Young dude that knew how to get money. One day, he came to me for 125Gs of coke and I figured I had a new customer and a good one. I wanted his business so bad that I fronted him the work every time he came. I came to realize that he was just fucking with me until his man got right again. But during this time, we started hanging out and I saw that he was a sponge to learn shit. I did not see that in too many kids born in the 80s. He became my main man. He knew how to earn but did not know where to put bread or how to be able to buy things he wanted. He was a diamond in the rough. I introduced him to the players in the area and it made him want more for himself. Everyone in Q.B. thought that he was working for me, but he was not. Sometimes I might make a point or two off him if he needed to get drugs, but when he began to come straight to me, the majority of the time to get drugs, I just did it for nothing. I made no money because we always knew that once in a while, his guy would have something and he would not charge me either. His guy having shit was few and far between. I pointed my man in the right direction for real. Started taking him to Vegas. Well, let me not say taking him. It was on his own dollar but he never experienced that type of shit before. We lived in Sin City which is to me, the greatest strip club in the world, located in the Bronx NY. Me, Manolo and my man Boulder from Q.B who is also younger than me. I knew him for years he was my man Sherman's peer. They ran the streets together as youngsters whenever Sherman was not in jail.

Boulder was also a hard worker in the hustle game and had his hands on many, different drugs. He went in and out of prison a couple of times and he respected me because I was always ready to give him a helping hand when he came home. When droughts came, my Chinese man seemed to always have work. His prices were high but he had it when none was around. Shit the highest I paid for work was 44k. The highest I sold work for was for 50. Dudes complained when half of them got it on the arm from me and they never considered that I had to pull 44k out to get the work to keep the streets moving. Selfish motherfuckers on the streets. I had been in the game for three decades at this time. I was around when birds were selling for 17 grand all the way up to when they were selling for 44k. I have been clubbing when bottles were selling for 60 dollars all the way to when they were selling 300 to 400 a bottle and this was regular. I have truly seen times and the game change and was able to stay afloat with it. I went from running out of deodorant and using my sister's secret, to buying nothing but 85 dollar Gucci deodorant. I am in jail, shaving with this bullshit razor but in the world I use a 300 dollar razor that I bought from "The Art of Shaving" store in Lenox mall in ATL. I came a long way baby! Anyway I pushed Boulder and Manolo. When the droughts came and they could not afford a kilo, I would take whatever money they have and put it with mine and buy the bird and break them off the piece for the money they had. I had to do this because when kilos got too tight connects would not sell open work. You either had enough for the whole thing or got nothing. They did not care if you had enough for 300 grams or half a kilo. All or nothing it was!

So I got them rolling with me traveling to the All-Star game. All the fights in Vegas and ringside I might add. My home girl got us half season tickets behind the backboard at Barclays when the Nets came to Brooklyn. My Chinese man and Shotta also had them but full season. As a matter of fact, for three seasons because that's what you have to buy without the hook up that I had. My Chinese man sat courtside. His two seats were 70k a year. So for the three years, it was 210K. My nigga Shotta came out to about 75k for three years. I travelled a lot if not with Manolo and J-Rock, it was with my cousin from Far Rock, Looch. Him and his huge GIB click were raking in the dough in Far Rock and down in Charlotte, Young Boys. They came up quick buying Benz's and trucks, jewels and partying around the country. At one point, I myself bought work from Looch. He had a good line and sometimes just to make sure that Chinese man was not just trying to rip my head off with the prices, I would get shit from someone else. I had to keep my Chinese man honest. I was getting kilos from Looch for cheaper than my Chinese man at times and like they say, Looch line for drugs came and left along with my man Ron who also was cheaper but his line came and left. But my Chinese man, he was serious having endless work. I mean there've been rare times he was dry and I even got shit for him but that was very rare.

Ooh yeah! I remember when Looch and his man Justice brought their first kilo. They were around 16 years old. They came to me and I told them to meet me at my sister's crib in my project. They came and I got my man Butch to see them. This was a big deal and they were young. We talk about this often and joke that neither side of the people involved in that deal gave me a dime. I committed a felony favor for nothing. Hey that's the way the streets work.

So now I got Boulder and Manolo ready to spend. We were buying Rolexes and cars and the hood wasn't feeling these dudes blowing up. Jealousy is rampant in the hood. Boulder was hesitant to buy a nice car, but Manolo was not. My Chinese man was now blowing out the water; Porsches, Benz's, BMWs, Challengers, two Jeep Cherokees, Range Rover which he had to pay 10k extra to get the car because they were so backed-up in pre-sale. Shotta was blowing up also. BMWs, SRT Cherokee as well as Manolo who had the new 550 BMW and a Grand Cherokee and was working on the four door six. Boulder finally caved and bought a truck. My last two joints were the new Infiniti JX60 which I was the second person in New York City that had one on the streets and I had the new ML Benz. Life was great for all of us and it seemed like it was only getting better. To some people, all of this would be overwhelming but to me it was a regular life because I was balling a long time. I was going to Vegas since '96. I was at the Tyson vs. Holyfield fight sitting ringside. The first fight.

It's 2013 and I was turning the big 40. I wanted to have a big party to celebrate. I host a party mostly every year because life is precious every year you make it in this kind of life. This one, I decided to throw a monster event. One night Manolo and I went to the Forty-Forty nightclub to hang out on a weekday. We ordered two bottles of ACE of Spade because the fucking place looks like an ACE of Spades museum. Anyway by the end of the night they were asking us did we want to become members of the club. Told us we could be gold or platinum members. Showed us the perks which were kind of good. I choose to become a gold member. In the package they give you a 40/40 hat, shorts, sweater and shot glasses. You also get to skip the line and never have to wait for a table with up to two friends whenever you go in there. You also get a 15% off your bill at the end of your nights there. I figured that was good if you come a lot. The price for membership was $3000 per year. You also get to have a party in the Jay Z suite one time for free. It clicked in my mind if they had my birthday available to use Jay Z suite then I would pass them the three grand. They had it so it was on. My 40th birthday would be at the 40/40 nightclub. The membership is also supposed to hold weight in all the other 40/40 clubs but that shit was not being honored. I will tell you that the party was great and when you get the room you have to spend at least 3k on food and drinks. Hell we turned it up! I had all the big players that I fuck with on deck. Chinese man spent probably 4k himself and I spent five, Manolo spent a few and my man Left who is Capone from CNN cousin spent a few thousand. All together we spent almost 20k in that spot that night and the manager respected that shit. My man Butch did not show up for the party so he and I went back a few days later with my man Thirty. Butch spent between five or six thousand in the spot on only ACE Rose and this was an empty night in the spot. Matter of fact they ran out of ACE Rose and Butch was beefing saying, "What if Jay Z shows up? What is he going to drink?" We laughed about that but Butch didn't let up because he owns a soul food restaurant and if he runs out of anything, the hood makes it out like he's the worst restauranteur ever. So he wanted to make me see and be clear that any spot can run out of shit even Jay-Z's spot. Okay Butch. I got your point bro.

A few weeks later we were back to 40/40 to watch game seven of Miami Heat vs. San Antonio Spurs. The place was packed. Celebrities everywhere. I am with my Chinese man, Manolo, Boulder, Shotta and my man Black. We have our table where I usually sit. They really treated me with respect in the spot and I enjoyed going there. We were eating and sipping ACE and Rose. During one point in the game, I went to the bathroom which is unisex. It was crowded up there and on the steps. I was climbing down the steps to head back to my seat. I bumped into someone. I looked up and it was Jamie Foxx. I say what up? He said what up. It was cool. I invited him to our table for a drink and he agreed. Boy! The look on my niggas face when I walked over to the table with Jamie Foxx and his man was priceless. I gave him a bottle of ACE for himself and passed him a few glasses and we started sipping and popping bottles all night. He called some women over and when I tried to pass them glasses, he said they couldn't use glasses. I was confused. He made them raise their heads to the sky and he poured the champagne in their mouths. Shit was wild crazy. Boulder got up and started doing the same to these bitches. We kept the bottles flowing. At one point, Jamie himself realized that people all over the club were snapping flicks of everything, but Jamie was cool with it. He kept having fun and taking pictures with me and my peeps and pouring ACE down the bitches' faces. He had on a Trayvon Martin T-shirt and we briefly spoke about the Trayvon Martin situation and he told me how he was going to make sure that the situation does not get swept under the rug. He also told me how Harry Belafonte told him that more actors need to stand up for the black community affairs etc. Jamie Foxx was a real dude. I told him that I would be in L.A. in a few weeks and that I would be attending the BET Awards show. He gave me his phone number and told me to call when I got there. He said he was having a party that weekend and I was invited. I really didn't think it would play out but I was cool with the night. I was hanging with the superstar on this night. He left with a bunch of people and me and my Niggas stayed.

My Chinese man had been flirting with one of the barmaids. So the club was getting clear so he decided to go to the bar to holler at her. On the way to talk to her he has an argument with a waiter. Next thing I saw him throwing a drink at the guy and then there was a lot of grabbing. I sent Black to go break shit up but by that time the bouncers were on deck so we all went to break shit up. There was a little bit of pushing and shoving. He ended up getting whisked to the side door and asked to leave. Before we did I calmed everyone down and told them to let us pay our last bill. I did that because I was a club member and did not want to fuck that up. We had already paid two bills, we could have slipped out but I decided to pay. The manager was there and one of the owners. The lady owner recognized that we were the dudes with Jamie Foxx. I paid the last bill for two thousand dollars and everything seemed calm and we left. I was tight at my Chinese man because he would have a fit if I fucked up something he brought me to so why the FUCK did he do this bullshit? Months later I came back to 40/40 and my membership was dead and I could not get in. The manager acted like the lady owner said if they let us in again that they would lose their job. I said that was bullshit. I did everything right from diffusing the situation to paying the bill. Fuck it though. At the end of the day, come to find out that the owner chick was a damn rat anyway. Why was Jay Z partners with her? She was mulling work years ago and got knocked and became an informant. That woman had some nerve curbing me when she knew the game but her spot ended up all over the newspapers in the whole A-Rod scandal. Fuck her!

So me and Manolo flew to L.A. and had a ball that weekend. We called Jamie Foxx and he answered and was supposed to meet up with us. It was a very busy weekend for him. His movie White House Down was coming out. We kept missing him but we stayed in touch while down there. We went to every event down there. We had a BET platinum package that cost 4K. Shit that was worth it. We went to the Kevin Hart movie premier. The list goes on. The BET package gave us gift bags with Moet, lotions, chocolates, roses, soaps all inside Samsonite luggage. That's the king of all luggage. We ran into my man Left down there and a few of our home girls from 10th street, who moved to Cali. We snuck them into a party where Nick Cannon was DJing. See, the parties were all exclusive. There was no paying to get in so if you didn't have that platinum BET Package you were out of luck. We had a ball at that party then we walked to a spot that overlooked downtown L.A. and stayed there for the night. My man Left had that crib out there. He used to be in L.A. with Ron Artest when he played for the Lakers and kept the crib after Ron stopped playing. The view was priceless. Next night, Manolo and I hit the awards. Crazy! We even walked the red carpet. It was included in the package. We had great seats and a few NBA players sat behind us. Celebrities were all around us. By luck when they were about to go commercial, the correspondent was sitting next to us and we were on national live TV on the 2013 BET Awards. Come the fuck on now! We are living! Those situations were being created because of the white powder we were selling. All phones start ringing immediately. Everyone is texting saying they just saw us. I was seen on TV before but not live TV and not on an event this big. How the fuck are we supposed to feel? How would you feel? No handouts, no being somewhere because you are on an entourage of a rapper. No yes man shit. This is real live hustle your way all the way to the top shit. During the show Jamie Foxx took to the stage and when he finished he hit my phone and told me I should leave the show now and get a car and head to his home because it was about an hour away. He said he needed our real names and there would be passes at the house for us. He gave me the address and me and Manolo rolled on out. We didn't want to arrive empty handed so we found a liquor store and grabbed a case of Veuve Clicquot Rose then we headed to the house.

The cab driver had to use navigation because he had never travelled in this area. This nigga's house is in a mountain with literally no neighbors at all. This mansion is everything you see in music videos and more. From the big windows to the cars parked out front to the super long Olympic style pool to the damn life-size dollhouse on the property for his daughter, to the music studio. I guess he had a sponsor because when we first got there everyone was drinking vodka. So when we popped champagne we stood out. At one point someone approached us aggressively and asked where we got the champagne. I told him we bought it for Jamie. He looked then laughed and said, "Oh, y'all the dudes from New York?" we said yes then he said we were good and to do what we want. He said he was in 40/40 that night with us. He showed us love. So now we were walking around popping bottles and everything, women walking up asking can they get a picture with me. Manolo was jealous. Jamie came through and gave me the biggest hug ever. Well, that is what it seemed like to me. He kicked it with Manolo and I for a few then said he had to mingle. It was real nigga shit. T.I. was there, Jeezy, Fab and every A-list black actress that you can name. I wandered into his studio and saw Snoop. Kurupt was in the booth who I was going to wait to holler at because I knew Kurupt for years. Kanye West was also in there. I asked Snoop did he want some champagne and he declined. I asked Kanye and he said "Hell yeah." I passed him the bottle and he popped it open. Before I could hand him a glass he took the bottle to his face. He tried to hand it back but I told him to keep it and I opened another one. I wasn't about to get into an argument at Jamie Foxx house with Kanye West. Now that would be going too far. The party was overwhelming. I remember finding a spot and just staring into the sky. Every time I do something that I feel I made it in my life something tops it. I've been shot 10 times, caught gun charges, assaults &robberies yet here I was at 40 standing in Jamie Foxx's backyard after I left the BET Awards. Wow I thought, that damn white powder. I had been to the BET awards before. I went to the second one when Monique hosted. That was a great experience even though we sat in the balcony where the people on stage say, "To all my fans up top, I love you." It still was great.

It seemed that if I wasn't stopped I didn't see any stop sign. By this time I was probably raking in close to 30K a month profit. No less than 14K so money was not an issue. I was standing there thinking what next? I need a legal business. I'm getting too old to keep up with this wild lifestyle. I played for all these years. Never snitched even groomed my family not to. In 2010 I was shot in the back and was in a coma for a month and in the hospital for half a year. I had six surgeries in two days. I was on my deathbed. My family knew who did it but no one told the police because they knew that's how I lived.

Well, I asked what's next. I was going to find out and soon. On the 29th January 2014 a narcotics task force ran into my home in Manhattan arresting me and my wife. Nothing was recovered in the house. At the same time, they ran into my friend Dash's house in Astoria, Queens recovering one unloaded gun and 100gm of crack. Also at the same time, they invaded my friend Nicole's house in Ravenswood also recovering nothing. We were all arrested and brought to Queens to be booked. The police confiscated five Rolex watches from my home, the Presidential 41mm, a Rose gold and stainless steel Yacht Master II, a stainless steel Deep-Sea Dweller, a 41mm Datejust II with diamond bezel diamond face and a woman's Datejust with diamond bezel. They took a 2013 Mercedes ML 350 and a 2013 Infiniti JX60. They charged me with major drug trafficking 220.77 and director of a criminal enterprise. Also weapons possession, conspiracy and drug possession. Mind you, of everyone arrested, only one unloaded gun was found and 100gm of crack. Dash and I got a 250,000 dollar bail a piece and the women got 50k a piece. It was crazy to me. I just ran down a lot of my life to you. Did I mention either one of them when it came to street shit? Hell no. See if the law wants you bad enough they will do what they feel is necessary to break you, I wasn't prepared for that move they made. Police had my phone tapped for a year and had me under video surveillance for eight months. They also had J-Rock, Boulder, Manolo and Dash's phones tapped. Boulder was arrested and was out on the 25K bail before I was arrested. When Boulder was arrested, we didn't think it was all connected or that phones were tapped. He got pulled over and the police found a loaded gun, 100 grams of dope and 20k in cash. When Manolo got arrested I figured I

was next because it was the same police that arrested Boulder and

we started to realize we were being phone tapped.

Manolo was stopped in Q.B. and they found 50 g of crack on

him. When they went to his house in Rego Park, they recovered four

guns, a silencer, 2 pounds of weed, over half a kilo of coke and 20K

cash. When I was picked up, again I said I had nothing and Manolo

had already taken a plea and was upstate doing his time already.

They charged me saying that I was everyone's boss. But that's part

of the consequences when you play this dangerous game of the drug

trade. The state or Federal government will try and crush you

totally. They said that the girls were involved and charged them

with conspiracy drugs and weapons. They charged the women for

fear and leverage. At the first court date the girls had ACDs on the

table but could not get them until I pleaded out. So in other words

Checkmate they had me. J-Rock, Boulder nor Manolo was on my

indictment but I was charged as their boss. They also confiscated

Boulders truck, Manolo's Jeep Cherokee, BMW 550 and his GMT

Rolex. Yeah shit hit the fan, the game was over. They tried to get

$1,000,000 bail for Dash and me but my lawyer who I love dearly worked her ass off and got it down to 250,000 dollars. I got bailed out as well as the girls on the case. The case was complicated and complex. I fought for eight months and ended up with two flat two post and a year for conspiracy. I copped out up to drug possessions which I had none and conspiracy. Dash got the gun tossed and got 2 ½ years and 2 post. The girls' cases were dismissed. Manolo ended up getting five years five post. Altogether the police did a investigation for over a year and charged me for it. I had to eat something so I did. In total, the state took five cars, six Rolexes, one diamond bracelet, about 40k cash, and recovered 100g of dope, over half a kilo of coke a few pounds of weed, 150g of crack and six guns.

Now I am writing from jail waiting to go to prison. I'm not sure which way to go from here. I have to try something legal. I feel that I can get on top no matter how I do it. Just need to refocus now. I never had time to do that because I was living the fast life. So many people died along the path of my journey. So many people caught long prison terms on my journey. I played the game and now I feel it's time to back out. Nothing lasts forever; you just have to know when to pull out before it's too late. For me it's not too late because I am going to get another shot. There've been plenty of hustlers that made way more money and accumulated way more items than I did. But not too many live the good life for as many years as I did. I made millions over my run. I saved money but probably blew more than I saved. Some money had to be spent for bails, lawyers, expenses etc. The real question comes back to why did I go this route? We have to look deep into why.

PART II

Progression

&

Understanding

There've been times as I got older that I wanted to exit the life. I knew that this life comes to an abrupt end. I have a cousin that was a financial advisor and now is a Branch Manager of a TD bank. We had discussions about money all the time. Here he is, educated from college with this great job and always complained about money. He drove a Benz; he had a Range Rover, two through his working career. He always says to me that to make 100k a year that you should not be driving a Range Rover or a Mercedes Benz. It baffled me when he would say that type of shit to me, but if you understand numbers, you would see why he says so. He always explained that making 100k, you take home sixty-something after taxes. If you live in New York City, you shouldn't drive a car that costs you a yearly salary or even more. Simple math. He also emphasized that if you hustle and bring home 100k, you would have to have a job in the "real world" grossing close to 130k or 140k a year. These numbers always discouraged me from trying to get into the workforce. I knew I did not have the education to land a job that made 140K a year, and I was getting too old to go and get that education. I also knew that jobs were decent but not designed to make anyone rich, let alone wealthy. I wanted riches for myself as well as for my family and friends. From riches hopefully we could turn it into wealth. After our discussions, I felt the streets were my best option to be able to do the things I wanted and needed to do. I had a lot of people to help over the years. I was the guy who, when people are in a jam, they came to for 10 bucks. Even people who I felt had good jobs. Of course they did not understand numbers so most of them lived way beyond their means.

New York City is a monster. Everything is expensive. It is a city that destroyed the middle class and is running the minority out of the city. It is becoming a place where you are either rich or poor. We didn't have many people pushing the Blacks or Latinos to have shit. I mean Rev. Al and Black Lives Matters cannot do it on their own. Rev Al. follows the steps of Martin Luther King Jr., who was a great man and helped our people a lot. I went to the 50th anniversary of the March on Washington. I support our history. I realized that just because we have a black president, we haven't won the struggle. White people want us to be happy and act like we are equal now. It's not the case. Not long before I was born, women could not vote and black people had to use separate bathrooms and sit at the back of the bus. I am not fooled because we have a Black president now. They constantly put propaganda on the news to bash him, to destroy the president's legacy. He pulled the troops from war, he killed Osama Bin Laden. He provided Affordable Health Care. The haters keep trying their best to sweep that under the rug. Well, Black people, let me be clear to you, he's the first and the last Black man we will see in this country as president if we don't vote. It might seem that I am getting off topic but I am not. We need leaders like Malcolm X and the Black Panthers again. Why? Because just like other countries do when there are conditions they don't like, we need to have a threat of civil war in our own country.

The logic is that nobody listens to talk not backed up. Everyone understands the universal language of violence. I also don't think we should blame White people too much because they are born thinking they are better. They are taught this at birth and in history books. I will never make excuses for a Black child not doing well in life, and blame it on White people, but that doesn't mean I don't understand that the white child has an advantage from the start. We were brought here as slaves. Most institutions in this country are owned by Whites, and they were created way back before the Blacks could own anything. So how do you think the playing field is even? These are a few reasons I never stopped hustling. It was an "illegal" business but it was mine. Through music, sports and films we have billionaires that are Black and we can make a change, but we don't. Why? I figure one reason, is that it is so hard for a Black man to get to the top, especially in the legal world, that they're not quick to share the riches with people. They figure get your own, from working like they did. The bottom line is that Black people are selfish because it is so hard to get their riches. Is it right? If these multimillionaires and billionaires really made decisions for our people, the Blacks and Latinos could start building wealth and not just be temporarily rich. If they did that, few people would hit the streets to hustle and less black people would be discouraged about life. We need to pool good money together and be the actual face behind the banks, the record companies, the sports teams. I know for a fact that Oprah, Jay-Z, and Diddy could open up their own banks. I also know blacks would use them. I also know they all know that institutions are built in a way which Black people get stumped and cannot get help because of the things that probably happened when they were young or debt passed to them. I'm not talking to them; I'm just using them as examples. No excuses, but the facts are it's harder for us than the Whites.

When a Black man does something that White people don't like, a new damn law pops up banning the shit. This goes back to the need for us to vote, vote, vote. We also have to change our mindset from thinking that we don't "deserve" shit or that other people are "supposed" to have stuff and we are not. This type of thought is a disease in the urban ghettos. We really think that without sports or rap music we are not going to make it. If I had the money or achieved the level of success that others did, I don't know if I would have done the things I am talking about but I would like to think so. Just think about it. A few years ago Diddy was the richest Black man in America. That shit was crazy to me, not really because it was Diddy, but because he was only worth $550m. I say only, but that's ridiculous money. I was just thinking like, There are no 'Black billionaires in the USA,' It made me think that there was no way I could stop hustling. Shit! That's the only way I was going to get my piece of the pie. And I did not even want to eat that much pie! Don't get it twisted. There are Black billionaires in the world, but only a few. It's now 2016, there are black men in the USA worth a billion and you know Oprah is way over that. Let's be clear also that Diddy and Dr. Dre are businessman. Not just rappers. 50 Cent is a businessman as well as Jay-Z. As just rappers none of them would have amassed the riches that they have. I am saying that becoming rich as a rap artist is slim to none. There are people that you know that are probably rich like your favorite rapper, but how many people rap? It's probably too many to count. Being and staying rich from rap is like your chances of making it to the NBA or even less because I believe way more people are trying to rap. Blacks need to become businessmen. At least I can say I was. I never got caught up in the hype of being a rapper and I was around a lot of them. I'm not saying you become an illegal businessman but a businessman. Educate yourself before it gets too late, well, before you think it's too late to educate yourself and you make a bad decision.

Everyone has to deal with their decisions and there is no reverse in life. No rewind button, no pause. Yeah, the legal way is hard but I am proof that the streets are hard also. Would you rather struggle or die? Do you want a one bedroom or a prison cell? Do you want a headache from struggling or body ache from gunshots tearing your body up? It's your choice. Don't be like Kane in "Menace to Society" and make the decision as your life is draining out of you. I remember years ago watching Jay-Z's "The Streets Is Watching" DVD/movie. I analyzed the year it was and what he had on, what he was driving and everything they were doing. At that time, I said to myself, "Shit! I am doing just as good as them or maybe better from what was shown on the DVD. Plus, I used to be at the Palladium and other clubs and see them here and there when I used to go out with Shameek and L.A. from Lefrak. L.A. was a really big spender. I heard he turned bad so I'm not condoning his actions, just telling it as it was. They were not doing anything I was not doing, so I figured I would stay in my lane. I always figured if guys were in the streets doing as well as they said they were, why the fuck would they start rapping? The pay was not great; it was more fame than fortune. After all, I grew up with some of the greatest ones and I knew how the industry worked. 10 years later, I looked up and Jay-Z's become a giant amazing man in his field of work. I thought, "Damn, this nigga blew up!" I thought that I had missed the legal boat! I was still getting money but I had to feel like I did not see the vision that some dudes had. I am not mad but I wish I would of at least Piggy-backed off the music on the business side because rap was one thing that belong to us. The Black man's insight is a mother, but you have to understand when to move on to the future. After thinking about it, I came up with that "number amount." It was something I figured I could get if I had a few more years. Two million dollars cash. That was my number. I had to have the round robin though. Meaning the jewelry, watches, homes, cars and 2 million in cash. Maybe if I thought of the number back in the late '90s or early 2000s. I could have achieved my goal then backed out and did something else. Maybe I would have bought fewer cars. I bought damn near 40 over my run. That's almost a car for every year I've been on this earth. Maybe I would have taken less trips around the country and out of the country. Or maybe I could have been trying so hard to get that money that I would've got knocked off in a year or two and did 10 years, or caught a murder and been doing life in prison. Hey, I've got to accept the cards the way they played for me. My mind is racing and words are just pouring, from my soul to get these opinions of mine along with the facts of my life to the masses of people that are willing to listen. My life is great whether I'm rich or poor because my mind is free even when I'm locked up. You cannot take away memories. That's why I will never forget all my friends who died at the hands of gunplay or all my friends in jail because of gunplay and/or drugs. I also think that people should respect the game to the point where they know if they shouldn't be in it. It's not to play with. I always said to myself "God meant me to push a Bentley," one of Biggie's lines that my man Cormega loved. I believe that line for myself. There are many ways to achieve that and I will use this time to figure it out. I could write my whole life story again and go down other vicious roads that I didn't go down or other situations that were left out. If you know people that know me, they may know someone involved in each situation I spoke about. Check court records; ask questions, because as I write this, I cannot believe the damn life I had up until now. I am 41 years old and have a long life ahead of me. I read a book that said most men don't receive their greatness until after 40. Look it up. Check the age of the billionaires or great men and see when they were at their peak. Lastly, the person that put me here is ME, I will turn this negative to positive. I won't let this weird kind of blessing be wasted. The great Buddha said that "suffering is the way to enlightenment" this experience is my blessing in disguise.

Let me tell you how ironic things can be in life. Here I am running around being this highly regarded hustler and being proud of my accomplishments. Happy that I've met the people I have met during my rise in the game. People knowing and fearing me in the record industry for random acts of violence they have seen me commit or heard about me committing. In my lifestyle this is prestigious. I cannot say that my acts of violence didn't gain me power and respect within different walks of life. I handled this respect as gracefully as I could. I always tried to work out problems through discussion before violence as I matured in the game as I became a bigger fish. I was doing so believing that staying free from unnecessary violence would keep the law off my back. I probably started thinking this way too late. In hindsight, I had a target on me and an infamous name running around the local precincts. So as I'm sitting in my cubicle one day and pick up the latest issue of Forbes magazine, either the November or December of 2014 issue and read an article about Steve Stout. I was in awe! Here is a guy that I met as just a rap manager for Nas. I had a small altercation with him which might have altered Cormega's career. Then Nas and Steve split for whatever reason. I knew he went into marketing but to what extent I didn't know and really didn't care. I kept advancing in my drug dealing situation and was moving in my own lane. Back in 2006 I ran into him at the 40/40 club. I was with a few dudes and was sipping champagne as usual. This is before they renovated 40/40 so I was sitting at the top of the stairs in a small lounge area by the back bar in perfect view to see any entertainer coming up the stairs to hit one of the back VIP rooms. Beyoncé was there that night as well as A-Rod. Steve Stout came up the steps and we spoke briefly. It was cordial conversation and I knew he was well off but not aware of exactly what he did. At the time I was at 40/40 with my cousin Shamel trying to promote my nephew Jay Rich to get a record deal. My cousin wanted to be in the music business badly. I mean BADLY! He loved the lifestyle that entertainers live, somewhat like my lifestyle but without the risk. He saw me and Stout converse and thought he should give him my nephew's music. I said "no". Shamel felt that the reason that we were there was to meet someone that could plug us in. I told him that I hadn't seen Stout in years and he respected me for what I did and who he thought I was. If I was in 40/40 handing out CD's for an unknown artist it would kill all my credibility with this man. Also, in my conversation with him it seemed to me that he was surprised that I was still alive. I felt like he thought the way he knew me to be I would have been dead or in prison. It was not the time or place to speak to him about my nephew's music. I just wanted him to see I was still around and doing well for myself. Of course he was a man that if he wanted to he could get the music to someone important but like I said, if he wanted to. I wasn't concerned about how he felt about the Madison Square Garden incident because there was another event downtown where he had a party and my friends and I got into a fight that turned into a gun battle on behalf of Stout. He asked me to help his brother or friend out and I did so putting myself and friends in harm's way. So I figured we were cool and had a decent amount of history.

Now fast forward to my cubicle where I am doing prison time and he's getting interviewed and talked about in Forbes magazine about making multi-million dollar deal with some tech-billionaires sipping champagne to their dealings. He came from being a rap manager of Nas to this giant in marketing. Hard work paid off. He's a great success story. This man and I have crossed paths on a few occasions but I just had the street mentality in me. I wanted quick money and was willing to do any act of violence for respect and power. Again, maybe if my mind was focused on a legitimate business I could have seen the fruits I had in front of me to make a ton of money. I know a lot of celebrities, I could have gone to either a small or large company and tried to get some type of marketing or promotion deal with the people I knew. I might have had to run around a lot or get a few doors slammed in my face or even been struggling for a while but it could have paid off. People always say that they never had this opportunity or that opportunity, well sometimes they are there and you just miss them because you're blinded by the street lifestyle. The managers are like clowns to the people that are hustling and running around with the rap artist or athlete etc. They have to run errands and get yelled at etc., but look how Stout ended up. Look how Don Pooh ended up. He was Foxy Brown's manager, another good dude. I still ran into him after

Foxy's situation at Def Jam ended. We ran into each other and a few star studded events like the Mayweather fights in Vegas or at the All-Star weekends each year. We stayed cordial and just acknowledged each other. I remember All-Star weekend in Texas one year he had a big party that I attended. He left me passes at the door. The who's who was in attendance! It was a Vegas themed party. Mary J Blige was one of the invited guests. When she showed up at the party security threw everyone out of the VIP area. A small commotion occurred because there was a bunch of high rollers from South Carolina in there. After the commotion was settled, Don Pooh allowed me to be one of the guests that stayed. That's where I sat and mingled with Mary and her husband, Kendu. I opened up by sending them a bottle of Nectar Rose where we sat and mingled while putting back a few drinks. We took a few flicks for my sister, who's the biggest MJB fan, and just sat and talk for a few. The night was cool! Again, I ran into Don Pooh in NYC at Sin City night club where I sent him a bottle of Grey Goose to show mutual respect we had whenever we bumped heads at these venues. That night I found out he no longer was involved in the music business but now owned a few businesses. If I remember correctly, I believe one was an

IHOP restaurant. I was probably bent that night! The point is he came from managing a rapper to being a prominent businessman. These are stories of men, Black men, minority men, that pulled themselves up from the bottom. Ordinary men just like you and I. These aren't men like LeBron James, Carmelo Anthony or Michael Jackson that have extraordinary talents. These are men that you look in the mirror and see every day. These two men are the "American Dream" ....

People like Cory McKay (Cormega), Victor Santiago (NORE) and Kiam Holly (Capone) are examples of how a second chance at a young age can change a person's journey and life. All three were arrested and sentenced to prison for shootings or robberies at young ages. After overcoming the obstacles of being in prison at young ages they came home and focused on their music careers. CNN, Capone N Noreaga became household names in rap music. Cormega signed to Def Jam before going independent and made songs with everyone from Lil Wayne, Styles P, Carl Thomas, CNN, NAS, Foxy Brown and host of other great MC's. Are any of the three rich? They all live comfortable lives in the field of Rap

Music. An honest living from following their dreams and focusing strictly on their craft. Some people will discredit the success of these rappers, but what's wrong with earning a decent living doing something you love? This love that they have has allowed them to travel the world. They've been to countries they probably would never have seen if they didn't "work" in the field of "Rap Music". Their jobs have helped educate these men. Educate them by allowing them to see and feel other cultures. To appreciate and learn other lifestyles. I applaud these men. Coming from our own war-torn neighborhoods they couldn't have asked for more out of life. When I first got my passport it was because Cormega was taking me to London to do a show back in 1998. He was doing a show with Brand Nubians and I believe Smith-N-Wesson that was down with the Boot Camp Click. It was the first time I saw steering wheels on the right hand side of the car. It was when I started to understand why there was a clothing line called London Fog. It was very dreary and foggy over there. Just remember all education doesn't come in a classroom, work toward being able to experience all fields of education. From the classroom, ghettos of our neighborhoods and traveling across the world and seeing first hand that the world is way bigger than just what's going on in the housing projects to the prison cells.

I am one of those firm believers that if you work hard for your money you will be less likely to blow it. I believe that you would appreciate it more and have a better understanding of money. My understanding of money, living within my means helped me live the blessed life that I lived. Of course, there are more things to do in life that I didn't touch but I understand that any part of 'rich' you obtain, there is a next level of toys made for people that have more money than you. They have things for the rich, super rich, the wealthy and super wealthy. So for that reason, set your goals and do not try to keep up with the Joneses. Shit in my line of work, do not try to keep up with the Meeches of the world or the Escobar's etc. Understanding money, I know that you can make one million dollars a year and still live check to check. It sounds crazy but it's true. People make more money and lust for more things, cars, bigger, more expensive ones. Yachts, jets, islands and countries! I could make any modest amount look like something. I remember when I had 300 bucks in my stash, taking packs from older guys and wanting to get to 10,000 to end my drug career. Now that might sound crazy but it's still plenty of dealers who never seen 10k at one time in their life and probably have given between 3 and 10 years of their life to the prison system trying to survive in the drug game. I always counted my earnings by the month. When I was making 7 to 10 grand a month profit for my pocket, I felt I was doing well. Keep my bills low and I would have plenty of room to save and buy plenty of luxuries monthly or yearly. For example, keep bills at 4k and make 10k. You have 6k extra a month. Since my plan was always longevity that would have been a good situation for me, I would pay my bills which is the mortgage/rent whatever and car payment if I had one and still save between 40 and 70k a year. After 10 years take out balling on your budget money and after that you could save about 350k. That's after paying all your bills and blowing 350k. Now when I up my profit to about between 20k and 30k a month but keep my bills still at 4k a month, what the hell type of shit do you think you can do with that type of money? Now we talking over 10 years 2.5m to 3m dollars minus the half a million for bills. That type of money in the hands of someone responsible is more than enough to live great. It is also small enough that you can stay under the radar of law enforcement. Shit I don't think the money got me investigated, I believe it was the run that I had. The constant look of the great life for so long when there weren't many people seeming to live that well in my neighborhood like back in the eighties and nineties when I could have blended in. If I sold between 2 and 4 birds a month, that would be between 10 to 32,000 bucks in my pocket or maybe more if there was a drought and I could raise the price per gram up to a ridiculous number. See, I look at money the way the government does. Understand to work a legal gig and bring home 200k you would have to have your bachelor's degree at the least and maybe even a PHD. After you are taxed, you still would only bring home about 130k of that 200k salary. If you change that up to drug dealing and you pocket 200k, you would need to have a legal gig that you made 275k. The government looks at what dealers gross not net and they charge you that way. It is not their problem if you see 1% or 10% or whatever off the amount you purchase. It's very important for hustlers to understand that so you can weigh if what you're doing is worth the punishment. Example if I sell three kilos every month, they say OK. Kareem paid let's say 35k for each. So he spent 105k a month, which is 1.26 million dollars a year. They go into what they feel you profited throughout that year. If they say you made 20k a month, that's two million, forty thousand a year. If you don't know who, what, why, where, that money went, it doesn't matter. Shit you could have made one sale to a undercover and borrowed money from people but they said it was all yours and you spend 200 to 300k, they will come a year later and say you did that every month making you look like this multi-millionaire drug dealer. They don't care about bills, losses, expenses or anything. They will just put your black ass away for as long as they can. Kinda scary if you're a middleman. Bargainer of some sort. You end up with charges you never thought you would get. Federal agencies you didn't even know exist are knocking at your door. These are things that are unspoken in this crazy drug game that we play. Like in anything you do you must do your homework. And not just look at the situation from the outside where you just see the glitter and glamour. Know everything about the business you're going into before you try and open up. See, because for you not to do so in the legal world, you may just lose some time and/or money but in the drug game, you can lose it all. Time in prison, or even your life. Your family's life can be destroyed, which is what almost happened to me. The police came and involved my wife who had nothing at all to do with my drug business. I didn't even know her when I started and by the time I got with her, she didn't fully know what I was doing. She was a hardworking woman making her way through college to get her master's degree. The wiretaps surely could have proved that neither of the women arrested on my case had anything to do with the streets but they locked her up unlawfully to leverage me to take a plea bargain which I eventually did. They thought they won but it was a blessing in disguise.

One of the biggest things my father ever gave me was a drinking problem. It is weird how I did not start drinking until I was 19. But when I did, I continued until this day. Doctors would say that I have a problem, and a serious one considering the amount I can consume. And you must consider that my father's side of family has a history of alcohol abuse. In a society other than the one I was involved with for the last 20 years; my drinking would be too much. In MY world, the underworld at the time, drinking and smoking weed is the normal. Some people in my "World" would also say I drank too much, I guess, but I did not feel it was a problem. They also had no problem drinking with me, while I was not one who smoked weed. I began to drink champagne a lot at 19, right before going to jail to do one year on Rikers Island. My friends and I would drink mostly every day. It's funny how people drink for the good times and for the bad times. I have always wanted in on the alcohol business. We would stand on the block where we had our 24 hour hustling situation going on and drink Moet by the caseloads. If the night was especially making a lot of extra money, we would step the champagne up to Dom Perignon. We were young ballers. We would drink and make money and have guns scattered around the whole block just in case someone tried to stick us up or any random situation that could occur in the projects. The drinking fueled me at times and gave me a carefree attitude about violence, women, and at times my values, principles, and morals. Sometimes, in fact many times, I have regretted the night before. At other times, I welcomed the feeling that this drink put upon me. The bottle symbolized a sense of success that not just anyone could obtain, where hundreds or even thousands were spent on champagne standing in the middle of the housing projects where most people are poor. The love among the people living in the projects was spread around in celebration with monetary gains and with plastic cups filled with Rose or XO Hennessy. The liquor also let me escape the constant nerves that you have from this life trying to stay one step ahead of the police.

Whether it is bad cops, plain clothes cops, task forces or the Feds, you must be aware of all the law enforcement. Neighborhood snitches who inform the police of what they see going on in the neighborhood. The alcohol keeps you relaxed and with that nonchalant attitude but also on point ready to strike violently. The alcohol could turn you into a beast you never knew you were. Under the influence, little problems became big or big problems became attempted murder or even murder at times. Sometimes, when people deserve to be shot or injured according to street law, the alcohol gives the aggression or the little extra push needed to follow through with what needs to be done. The flip-side is that the alcohol can have you pushed to the murder level when the situation does not call for that under street law, leading to the aggressor feeling guilty, or afraid of the consequences. This one drug is complicated and is represented in so many different aspects of street life and in "regular" society also. Alcohol to me in the nineties was like what cocaine was to hustlers and young professionals in the late seventies and eighties. Studio 54 cocaine use represented success as a user. Hey you can pick your poison. Alcohol, tobacco, cocaine, and heroin: they all can destroy a life but the ones that the government cannot regulate are what they keep illegal. The ones that cause more physical harm to your body, they keep legal because there's big money in it. Tobacco cartels and alcohol cartels help people get elected. By their funds, they help people run big campaigns which help them win elections and build governments, so laws will always be in place for these cartels to grow. Yes, I call them cartels if that is what they call suppliers of cocaine, and the suppliers of heroin. Like I said, pick your poison. Alcohol kills your body and the use brings out feelings and emotions to have someone kill somebody else, yet it is legal. Then to put more money into the companies' hands and government's hands, they arrest you. If you drive at a speed that most people are not drunk at, which causes jails to fill up, lawyers to be hired, bails needed to be paid, fines etc....I can tell you one thing: the government is crafty and strategic! I know times when people have shot others in the hood and they forget that they did it in the morning due to alcohol. This is the few that alcohol gets the best of.

I dreaded the days when I could not remember that whole night of drinking. This began right before I was arrested and began doing this prison time. So I'm not sure if that blackout was because of the drinking, or was the other factors like stress and fatigue and overthinking, add to it. I've never had a car accident while drinking but I do see how easily you can have one. You just don't know when that last sip could push you over the edge. At times, I couldn't remember how I drove home. I began to worry about this a little and wanted to slow down on the booze. I would slow down when I wanted but I was a socializer that had a lot of funds, so I knew how to make people happy when they came around. I was a people pleaser even if it was affecting myself or my family. I pleased them with 20 years of celebrating "just because", maybe because it was the weekend or it was fight night, game night, birthday, funeral, boredom, whatever. If people wanted to drink with ICE, I would buy. No regrets with the sharing though. I would also use these hours of drinking with schooling the young hustlers or telling the women about getting their lives together, whether going to school or taking the next city test that came out. Sometimes, I would spend those hours scolding people about how they were underachievers. Yeah, they hated that shit, but if the drinks kept coming, they kept taking the abuse. Most knew that I had their best interest at heart. I was like the mailman that you can count on for your mail every day, but you don't know if it was going to be a check or a bill. Hey, you have to open it anyway. I love my neighborhood. I love my life. I love to joke. Alcohol would bring all those thoughts and feelings out of me.

Everything I do in life I try to look at it from a view that others might not see. I set my mind to something and see it the way that I want to see it. The same thing goes for this prison situation. I look at it as a preparation to go back to the world. Most of the men here do not look at it that way. I see those cubicles as a workspace that most people work in that do not have offices. The dorms are set up in that type of format. They wake you at 6:45 AM every morning, as if you had a job in the world. Not only if you had a job in the world but even if you ran your own business or company. Why would you let your mind feel defeated the way they would want you to think? This is just the reception part of prison and you can end up somewhere that all your street situations can come back to haunt you. So the balance between you keeping your mind feeling that you are in a learning environment, and a war zone is hard at times. The officers are nasty and the food is no longer gourmet, but what the hell do you expect? For one I will give the officers a little room for error because a lot of the inmates are total assholes. Many of them are junkies that are disguising themselves among gangsters, drug dealers, robbers, and killers. They gain their weight back and portray that they are these strong men in the street, but their actions tell a different story. So being that so many of these men are this way, the officers have a tendency to treat all men informally, which is wrong but that is what happens. I too at times wish to break an inmate's skull for the childish ways they act in the dorms. I believe if I had more time to do in prison, my temper would spill over to the violence. I still don't know if by the time I leave this place, my temper won't get the best of me. I feel that if you have short time, you should have the patience to put up with most of the ignorance of the officers because you should look at it as if you're just passing through the prison system and it's not your home. You're just visiting. Long timers have to demand a different type of respect from staff and inmates. It's sad but true. I see men in here that are sorry excuses for men. No integrity, no moral values at all. Most of the men here do not use this time wisely. Always talking about going home but no plan on what to do when they get there. I see dudes leave day after day with no plans. Could men be this foolish?

I spoke to a young Blood gang member the other day and he told me about a situation where he was going to get paroled home to where he has beef with dudes in his project. They live in the building across from him in the Bronx Millbrook project. From his story it's over the guy's sister, whom he dealt with and the brother did not like him for whatever reason. This led to gunplay with him running from parole. He got caught and is now doing a violation of parole. This kid is 23 years old and has already done about 4 to 5 years behind bars. The problem with these guys is a bunch of bullshit but he does not know if it can be resolved without violence. He grew up with those guys. Childhood friends are now foes. I hope everything works out for him. These are the kind of things that put a people behind bars before they get to live. I told him to try to stay out of situations where the result is something that he cannot live with. That's one thing I always tried to do. Only put myself in positions that if the outcome ends in a life sentence or being paralyzed or shot, that I'd be able to deal with it. Don't kill someone for something that is small or something petty then get the life sentence, and only then do you recognize it as a senseless act. Again in this life, there is no reverse or let's start again. Myself, I can adapt to any situation because I can reason myself into being prepared for anything. I study the street life. I look at the guys that were good at it that came before me. Not only what they did on the streets, but also study how they handled themselves in prison. It's very important to look at both sides. When I was young there was a guy named Mike that was one of the neighborhood tough guys. He lived in Queensbridge at one time but moved down the block to Ravenswood where he hung with the Ravenswood's thugs. Shaheem, Mece, Raymond, Jayvon, Laymeek, Shameek, Freddy, Justice etc. They were always outnumbered when it came to having beef with Q.B. guys. I didn't know him because I was too young. As I grew up, he was hearing about me from prison and from keeping in contact with his friends from the neighborhood. I was a rising star and he was probably anxious to really be able to sit and kick it with me because his hood, Ravenswood was coming up as a neighborhood that was respected. Him and his crew were respected but to a limit. Queensbridge dudes would come and have their way with them sometimes, but once me and my friends (which are some of his old friends) put a foot down, things changed as if Ravenswood guys were the troublemakers.

Well, anyway, Mike got out of prison and we bonded. He was a great guy to meet. A tough guy and very humble. It was sort of a medal of honor to do time for murder in Elmira etc. in your teens and come home. One conversation he and I had that stuck with me all these years, was a statement that told me plenty about prison. He was not trying to grandstand about his murder or how tough he was, he let me know that I better be prepared for this life as a whole if I planned on playing it all the way out. He told me he thought he was a killer until he met some killers. That statement let me know if you think you're bad it's always someone badder. To me you can never be over prepared for what life will throw at you. Thanks Mike, I needed that. People should be afraid to come to prison. That should be the scary bedtime story that families tell the children at night. Not the stories about the ghost or haunted house, because all the damn ghosts are in the haunted houses which is these prisons! I wouldn't want anyone to have to come to this place. I joke with Manolo and call this facility "jail heaven "but it is far from that. This place brings grown men to their days of childhood. Prison makes grown men become dependent again on their mother and fathers for support as they did as children. Either that or it forces men to ask the women in their lives girlfriend, wives etc... for money and packages. Then when they are released back into society, people wonder why these men cannot function as the alpha in the relationship. And people wonder why these men turn into womanizers and become lazy. They are unconsciously trained to become this way from the time spent in correctional facilities. They send these men to learn trades while in prison, but it's more like a JHS setting. You are told to read chapters and answer questions at the end of each chapter. You find yourself skimming around the chapter just getting the answers. Not really applying yourself to learn the material because you're in class where everyone is on their own pace. The teacher just wants to see you working and to occupy time. I recall giving my question paper to the teacher and I grabbed back a sheet of scrap paper from the bottom and told him" oh its nothing" I almost handed you my scrap paper. He looked at me like I had six heads. It's like he couldn't fathom the thought that an inmate would really want to learn the work and get the answers right. From that moment I lost interest in the class. I mean I have my own agenda for what I want to do when I am released but to me all knowledge is good knowledge. It cannot hurt to know things. So why would I take a trade and just want to slide through until it's my time to leave prison? If I said it once I have said it a thousand times, I won't waste my time while doing time. It would be hard enough to keep up with the ever changing times that we live in while I am inside. Trying to keep up by reading papers and watching the news and listening to talk radio. If I just bullshit around I will be lost.

All nationalities are in prison looking for a better life. Are they really? Are they looking for the white picket fence or are they looking for the brick wall mansion? These dudes are here and won't take the time to learn the language here. How can you try to get ahead in a new country if you don't choose to even learn the language? Prison is a place with a large amount of people who would just want to make excuses for their lives, or who've taken a shot at getting to the top the fast way, and missed. For the ones that took the shot, I'm not mad at you, but if you get another chance, try a new route. If you missed that shot, don't let this jail time be wasted. Learn a trade or at least finish school or do something even greater like a guy Rell that I know. From what I am told, Rell learned fluent Spanish while in prison just from being with Spanish dudes. He did 10 years. That was how he made prison work for him and not the other way around. Don't get me wrong, there are a lot of brilliant men in prison, but they are hard to find. In the beginning of a guy's bid he has so much in his mind, like how he's going to do so much time or will he get out early. Will he have problems with the guys from either county jail beefs or street beefs? So they cannot apply themselves to finding the brilliance in themselves at that time. Once a person settles into his or her bid, they need to start focusing on what they will do when they get out. Most people are reactive and not proactive in life. Sometimes I look at my situation and feel that God keeps blessing me. You will ask why I would say that after all I've been through and I say because I know things will get better. This is just a stage, a part of me, another part of Kareem. God does not interfere with day-to-day life. I make my own "luck." All my situations, whether bad or good, I made on my own. It is as simple as that. Time will go by if I was dead or alive at the same speed. A person's time is empty and they fill it up with the things they do. Choices they make fill up their time, so how your day ends up is your own fault. I read something along my journey that said something to that effect and I believe it is true. So I can say that Kareem made his time count, as I am doing now by writing this which I hope, no, that I know will become a big selling book. My bunky, a guy from Sullivan N.Y. is laying in his bed with his coat over his head wasting time, and the big nose guy from Long Island is in the cube across from me making noises like a kid's TV show then, these men will be complaining that life dealt them a bad hand. Well, was it worse than Nelson Mandela's hand or Oprah Winfrey's hand? If you cannot think that huge, was your hand worse than 50 Cents' hand? Everyone can relate to the music mogul from South Jamaica that was in prison at one point but probably will never do that again. He spends his time now doing whatever the hell he feels like, but chooses to publish books, produce cable TV shows, write music etc. Why can't every one of us be like 50 Cent? It takes hard work and by lying in the cubicle, that's not going to cut it. Here I am in this place labeled a Central Monitory Case (CMC) so my movement to a prison where I can progress is being held up, but I cannot do anything about it so I will write. I will write and read and brainstorm, brainstorm, brainstorm, and write more until I hit the jackpot of ideas. If I get discouraged, I will write someone or call someone to get me back on track.

My co-defendant Manolo, even though he's not on my indictment, (he was on my arrest report as working for me) is a very big thinking guy. I stay in contact with him to see what business ideas or investments he is thinking about. Most of his ideas have already been done, but he keeps thinking of more and he likes to be secretive about them. I love his ambition. It reassures me that not all hustlers from the "bottom of the hoods" only think about, should I say "bullshit" all day? Some can flip some birds (kilos) of coke and pounds of marijuana and still think about having a clothes hamper with wheels to make it easy to get to the laundromat. Yes it has been done but the point was that he had never heard of nor saw one. So in his head it was an original idea. That's what makes him brilliant. Keep thinking of ideas lil bro. You went from Q.B. house to Jamie Foxx's house, brother's no fool! I made certain rules for myself when I came to prison, and certain goals. I insisted that I would write a book about my life and if it sold, great, if not, I would still have the title author under my belt, which is a great accomplishment to me. It's really strange how a few people can change communities. In the underworld, power shifts can happen in the blink of an eye, either by hostile takeovers such as murder or something as simple as a person moving out of the neighborhood and giving up his territory. The latter usually does not happen. People are too greedy in the drug game most times to know when to bow out gracefully. Most people need a little help from either the police arresting them or an attempt on their life, or the ultimate help out of the game is getting murdered.

Two of the three things up until now have happened to me but it did not convince me to quit the drug business. I've always felt I would be weak to quit on those terms, which under street law would be showing weakness. So I kept going. Luckily for me, I'm still able to be writing you this book knowing I will be on the street after I finish this short prison term. Many men did not and will not get the chance to tell their story anywhere except behind a prison wall.

Who wanted me out of the community? Let's analyze this question and see what makes sense. Would it be the people whose stores I bought products from and frequented every day? Was it the restaurants in the neighborhood where I bought lunch and dinner (and the most expensive meals on the menu), helping the business flourish? Could it be the barbershops, supermarkets, or dollar stores, where the dealers who work on the outside all day, spend hundreds or thousands of dollars a month? I would think if it is these people from the community, they don't realize how important myself and my friends were to the community. We got the buildings in the projects safe. We ran the would-be robbers out of the neighborhood. Sometimes it took violence to get this accomplished but in the grand scheme, we had the neighborhood flourishing. Children in the poor neighborhoods look for people to follow and get advice from and they cannot always look to their parents. They see a young successful hustler and they lean towards them for advice. That is where it can get tricky. On this situation, I can only speak for myself and my intentions.

Once again, I will say that I had many positive people in my life and I used selling drugs as a business to take care of my family just like a cigarette dealer does. So I'm saying that, to say that I wouldn't be a bad person for a kid to come to for advice. Why? Let me be clearer. First of all, I never wanted to or needed to trick anyone into selling drugs for me. Shit, the way I screened a potential worker was tougher than someone applying for many city or state jobs. People came to me for work and plenty of people have been turned down because of laziness, work ethic, thought patterns, aspirations, etc. If a young kid came to me for any advice, I would give them the best advice even if it did not advance me in my goals. My moral integrity keeps me from using trickery to add a worker to my company. For two reasons: one is because this job is just like being a cop or a firefighter and is not for everyone. And two: because you cannot get the best work from people who don't have the passion to be a good hustler or a businessman. Make no mistake, it's all business! I encourage kids to go to school, play sports, not to break laws, to dream big, be the best men and women of their world and many other positive things. They listen because they admire me. Yes, they admire my success in their eyes, not looking at my route but the results. So for that reason I have the power to dictate the direction the young kid travels, to a certain extent. Why not encourage them to be doctors, lawyers etc.? The Black and Hispanic community needs professionals that understand their own people. So I point them toward their strengths and will even help them financially to stay on the right path. Taking my friends and I out of our neighborhoods has a effect on violence in the community. The bad kids or underprivileged kids that resort to violence can sometimes be slowed down and stopped or saved from life in prison or death by the generals that they respect in the neighborhood. This is done hopefully before the police have to step in and find a reason to gun our youth down out of fear of getting shot or fear because they do not understand our community. We can police ourselves to a certain point and save misery for a lot of families. We know both sides of the beef going on in the streets and can possibly sit the groups down and get the situation settled without senseless violence. Not saying that all violence is senseless of course. Who can understand better than us? Parents call the cops to inform about the shootings and robberies etc., to protect their children, but the police end up coming into the neighborhood and killing the children anyway. Much of this can be avoided.

Remember one thing, drug dealing is bad because the government says it is bad because they cannot control it and profit from it. They hate to see male minorities become rich. Now add to it we don't have to get the same education they did to become rich. Drugs do alter people's thinking which can lead to other crimes but alcohol does also but is legal because THEY say so. Believe it or not, crime helps poor communities. It is known but most people would not want to say it. Crime also helps the rich. People who want private prisons, lawyers, doctors, police and other civil servant jobs all the way down to supermarkets, hair salons, barbershops and restaurants. Drug crimes feed all these industries and more. It's weird but taking certain dealers out of the community is killing the community. You'd have to live in such a community to understand. People who are unemployed for whatever reason stay afloat from crime in the poor communities. Answer this: what is the point of taking voting privileges anyway if you're on parole or probation? How does that benefit the community, if the people that live there cannot have a say? That forces them to commit the same crime they did to put themselves where they were. Back in prison or being poor. How does it benefit the community if a felon cannot get certain jobs just because he's a felon? I could understand if the felony shows in the background check, but the person still had a chance. If he does not get the position it should be because he is not qualified not because he has a felony. It keeps people in rat race, then you wonder why it is so much crime in our environment.

People choose to hurt themselves. You don't hold addicts down and make them use. Abusers abuse by choice. All I'm trying to say is that you should try to understand us before you judge us. Drugs were one of the best and worst things I ever came across. The power of drugs goes on both sides of the coin. It has the power to get the drug dealer rich and famous or rich and infamous. It also has the power to destroy lives to the point of no return. I used to think that people that use drugs were just weak and deserved everything that happened to them because of the drugs until I got involved in the drug game. And as I became an expert in dealing in the drug game, I came to see that I was absolutely wrong about the people. I have plenty of close friends, classmates, comrades, partners in the drug game that fell victim to drugs. Some have bounced back but many have not. I have a great friend that fell victim to drug use. We came up together, we are the same age but he had a harder life than I did growing up. One day, he told me he used and I turned my back on him. I vowed to never fuck with him again unless he was clean. When others found out, they didn't turn their back and even attacked me verbally for not being more understanding. Shit I don't understand. I didn't understand it. If I let him think I was OK with it, he would never stop it. I stuck to my guns. I gave him the cold shoulder because I knew it would hurt him because he valued our friendship. I also opened my eyes that the drug is strong. The strongest of all men can fall because I knew he was a strong man. He battled with his addiction for a while, in and out of programs and has now been in Mid-State prison for seven years. I love him to death and we were spending time together before he went to prison but I let him know that things couldn't be the same until he stops completely. He's a hustler and when he gets out, maybe we can put a business together for him to be able to be in some type of sales. He's also an excellent chef and a true friend. There's no way to mention my life without him being mentioned for our close true friendship.

Hustling drugs in other states was not really my thing. I probably could have made plenty of money doing so, but for the most part, I stuck with things I was familiar with. That was a good thing and a bad thing. When I think about it I dealt drugs the same way I attacked life legally. At times I was scared to pull the trigger on what was probably good out of town ideas. I did analyze the profit margins from buying drugs for low in New York and selling them super high in the southern states where the drugs were not as plentiful. That was back in the eighties, nineties and early 2000s because now with terrorism and things like that, the equation has switched around. Yeah, I said terrorism. You see, after 2001, New York City police had so much funding to protect the city it made everything harder to smuggle in. Even if the war was not on the drug smugglers, the technology was in place and drugs were getting intercepted also. So smart business was to just change the drop-off state. This is just business 101. So it flipped from New Yorkers bringing drugs to Atlanta, N.C, S. C., VA, to New Yorkers going to buy the drugs from Georgia and California hoping to get it back to make the mark-up.

Anyway, back when New York was one of the drug capital states, in our own country, my friends were cashing in. My man Spunk probably was the guy who I knew the best that made millions down in North Carolina. Spunk had a major run in N.C. hustling from city to city. Even though he was big time, he was able to stay under the radar for years. Even before he left Queensbridge Houses where he was from, he was making a bale of money. That's an expression my man College would use "Bale of money." I like that. I admired Spunk. He opened clubs, bought houses and seemingly had the drug dealers dream. I tried to have the same thing but from my New York flow. I got up with him every time I went to N.C. because it's just the thing to do. When people from New York are in your town that you know, you go out for drinks or parties. I myself was a hustler with a sharp eye, because people are not who they say they are. They act like they have a bunch of money but are "fraud willies" as Jay Z would call them. My man Spunk was not. Around the country at events I would run into him, and we would acknowledge each other's situation. People that were close to him would tell me that I reminded them of Spunk. I had no problem with that. I am a tough critic so when I was telling my cousin how Spunk was paid while my cousin and I were down in Miami one weekend, he was anxious to see and meet Spunk.

This weekend was a Memorial Day weekend so everyone from rappers to drug dealers was down there. I told my cousin that Spunk was with Nas and we would see them later that day. When we finally ran into them, Nas came with Spunk, Ocean, Super Ed, Germ, Jayson, Sleazy and a few other dudes from Q.B., some of whom use to be my best friends as a youth. It was great to have all of us down there mobbing this weekend. I also ran into Nitti and Webb, and my great friends Shotta, Maxi, Tiff, Mecca from Farmers and many other good people. Anyway, my cousin was not impressed when he saw Spunk pull up in a Chrysler PT cruiser. The car was definitely bullshit but I look at it as, damn Spunk been in the south too long. I mean he had an almost 30 year run without an arrest. My cousin thought that at the event Spunk would pull up in something big because of all the stories I had told him about Spunk's cars in the nineties from Drop Saabs, Q-45s, the Maxima when it first came out, Lexus etc. I too was surprised but knew that Spunk was getting money. He stayed in the same hotel as Nas. He had the Presidential Rolex on. He just looked like a country nigga now. Or did he run out of bread? He did open clubs then close them. Did the pressure to turn his success legal drain all his funds? People don't realize just because you have a long run doesn't mean everything is going great. It's harder to live on the street than in prison economically. You have house payments, car payments, business payments, lawyers, bails, multiple women, children to look after. Everyone has their hands out needing something. You have to factor in losses from drugs, money used to buy weapons, droughts etc. Me having a long run, I understand these things and not too many people stay afloat through all of the trials. He also threw the parties at his strip clubs with different performers to pay from Juvenile, Jeezy to Nas and Mobb Deep. So when he was arrested in 2012, it was big news to everyone in New York City and I guess N.C. also. He lasted through three decades of hustling but the game was now changing and maybe his focus changed a little. See the bad part about it is that once arrested, over 20 people popped up to testify about buying drugs from him over all these years. People were saying Spunk paid them to burn other peoples' clubs down so he would have no competition and Spunk did this, Spunk did that. After the trial, he ended up getting life in prison mostly based on shit people said he did years ago. Country people!

One of the biggest reasons I never wanted to go out of New York was because of the boys in the South that I did not grow up with and who will show no loyalty when the FEDs were on them. It can happen vice versa also, that a New York dude would be the one snitching, but this example is the country guys folding. Most of them were already in prison. See I could have watched Spunks rise and jumped on the out of state bandwagon like many around my way did but were not as successful and so they ran back to New York but I did not. I decided to stay small and stay steady. My man Tommy told me to stay small and keep it all. I understood and that was my play anyway. Spunk is appealing his case and hopefully he'll get a time cut. I pray for him and honor him for being one of Long Island City's best, and for being a stand-up guy. Those types of stories kept me in the city. A couple of my other friends from my projects followed suit with Spunk and went to hustle in N.C. and tried their luck. They also came up quickly, amassing huge sums of money. They called me the Poster Child of the neighborhood, meaning I set the standards for what you do when you get money. Well, if I was the blueprint, they followed it well. They made their runs and used to come back to New York to buy cars, jewelry, clothing, etc. Always made it back to New York if I was having a party or BBQ, and drop three to four cases of champagne. That's when cases were 12 bottles. This is when Biggie was hot they were loving Coogi sweaters. A string gets too lose the sweater is trashed. I was proud of them. Butch had a Benz buggy eye and his man had the RR. 4.6 or Jay Z would have shitted on him. It was cool and we all were just living out the life that we dreamed of and the stuff the rappers were talking about in songs. Butch man had the platinum chain when dudes had the white gold. Even me. A couple of dudes from the hood wanted to rob him when he came home at times but I would talk them out of it because him shining was all of us from our hood shining. Fuck the hate. We had the hood, let him do what he has to and come home to his hood and be able to take a breather. These dudes would have done it also. One of them ended up sticking Lamar Odom in our hood years later. Eventually, things happened down there and my man Butch came home but his man stayed. The FEDS ended up catching up to him and he folded. He snitched on some dudes. It's no excuse! He lived the life and he was not man enough to pay the price. He had bought a home, had several cars and had money. He claims some of the people involved ratted on him first, but that is no excuse and I know it and he knows it. With his cooperation, at least one person got 20 years. He ended up doing five years and came home and left the game alone. Dudes in N.C. want his head. Damn got all the money, but did not know the cost of the game. He broke my heart with the way he handled that situation. He's a guy that I grew up with and had a good heart. If I look back I can see he was more of a clever money getter than a gangster.

There are plenty of hustlers that think it's just about the rewards of the game. He had no excuse, he was not very poor. He had a two-parent household. He worked jobs before and he's working one now. Him and I spoke about his fatal mistake. I have a policy of not dealing with rats at any level. I can do my part to make sure that every rat I come across is uncomfortable and if one does it to someone in my camp, to deal with them accordingly. Even as children your parents scolded you for being a tattletale! It breaks my heart that he and I cannot be close like we used to as kids. We hustled together, ran up in a crack spot together, shared bullet proof vests, I borrowed tens of thousands from him when I was 20 and he never blinked about me paying him back (I needed the money quickly to buy a car. My money was not readily available). We were even picked up on a shooting together after a big shootout in my projects where a woman was hit in her hand. Now these type of situations build strong street bonds, but by him breaking the law of the street, broke the bond that was built by risking our freedom.

So again, I say the out-of-state money comes fast. My cousin Cash got out of prison after nine years served in Charlotte, N.C. for someone telling the police on him and my other cousin Looch and their New York crew who was out there. Cash took the weight and everyone else got off light. A stand up man from New York caught up in the south. My man Lord is being railroaded by some Ohio dudes. I really don't think the telling is because of demographics, I believe it's from not knowing people from these places from birth. When the police wave that time in front of dudes, they start to realize that they just met these guys a year or two or five years ago and they won't do life for them. Therefore I stick with who I know. I stick to what and where I know. These are qualities of the art of war. Oh yeah thanks to Zerena and Sherri for getting that work to the south (LOL).

One of the few times I decided to make an attempt in the south to make some money, I too ended up in N.C. The state is like heaven for New York hustlers. I ended up in Greensboro, North Carolina. It was cool because I had good people out there and a girl I love to go see and her family whenever I was in town. The small operation I did with my comrade Shotta and my man from Brooklyn that I met through my man Nut, named Flip. He was in N.C. doing his thing. He told me out of 50g of heroin, we could gross almost 30K. I thought this was impossible but was willing to entertain the idea. Shotta had the connect to get the dope for about 4K for the 50g. I really didn't know how Flip cut the work and it did not matter. He promised a certain percentage off every ten grams and he did as he said. The only problem was that it took almost the whole month for him to finish the work. Hey who the hell cares for that profit margin? Shotta and I drove down with a female who would hide the dope, which was easy to do since it was such a small amount. It went well for a while. Shotta and I had a lot of bonding time and learning about each other, we became much closer on these road trips. I used to listen to slow jams the whole route and used to explain the concept of the songs to him until he would give in and began to enjoy the music as well. Yeah, I had to school him. People figure "man we are running drugs up and down the interstate we need to hear some hustling music." I didn't care about that shit, we really were living the life in reality and we didn't need any attention drawn to us, not no rowdy ass rap music. Eventually, the route died out because Flip was taking too long to finish. It was cool though, no one took a loss and we ended things admirably. Real money was made. THE END. I love you Flip, always have and always will.

Now let's relate these situations to legal business. If we are willing to put the same hard work in and just take the shot, we could have an import-export business. We can apply to a business, the same principle as the drug game from which we really got the principles from. You are managing people, getting products to a place in a certain amount of time, replacing orders and networking with people. In the drug business, most people start small and build up clients and business. It's the same as if you started with a small business start-up. You can work diligently and build up clientele and boost sales and profits. Why are we quick to do something that looks to be easier, when in reality it isn't? Besides getting the licenses and permits for the legal business, it takes the same hard work to build your illegal business. In reality, you have to get permits and licenses for the illegal business. You get them from other street dudes that are going to be willing to let you hustle somewhere or will attack you to occupy your territory. In the legal business, if you don't get a permit, you pay taxes and fines and maybe lose your business but can try again. In the drug business, without permits you can pay with bullet holes, prison stints, or your life, which you definitely cannot get back. When looking at things through these eyes, the option to try the legal way makes most sense. There are obstacles on both sides but you lose less if you fail on the legal side. One of the toughest young men I know told a friend of mine on a visit as he is doing his

80 to life sentence that he wishes he wasn't the gangster he is considered to be. He said he is tired of the gang banging and wish he could start over. He wanted to apologize for all the people he hurt. He is 36 years old with 80 to life sentence with about 15 years in prison already. So people listen up good. Once decisions are made, they cannot be taken back.

Dash, my lil bro. There is so much to say about him. Even though he is 39 years old, to me, he is still a diamond in the rough. I say this because I see so much more potential in him than what has shone through up until now. I always loved him and kept him close. We've done a ton of crime together and this is the first time we ended up in prison stints at the same time. He's done about four or five bids, which don't add up to much because I've always produced lawyers for him and bail. This man never had to save up any of his own money for business purposes and he knew it. He's a ladies man, a great friend and definitely a gangsta. His house was raided one time years ago, and the police found a .45 Caliber and maybe 3K in crack and some money. His mother was at home at the time along with her friend and Dash was in his room. The police tried to leverage Dash, by telling him that they would not arrest his mother if he would just call me and tell me to come to his home for whatever reason so they can arrest both of us for the drugs and the gun. They made this request in front of his mother who was scared and pleaded with him to make the call so she could be let go. Dash felt sorry for his mother and angry that they would make a request to him like that in front of her. Dash knew the rules of the game and told the detectives "Hell no!" He then turned to his mother and told her, "Mom, it's going to be a long night." Most people would have called their friend, boss, whatever in a heartbeat to save their mother but Dash stuck to the code of the street which people think doesn't exist anymore. This occurred in the nineties, and over 20 years later, Dash and I were arrested together and this time they were charges that hold life, and no one bent over again. We were true G's in the life of the street. We go way back since he was 15 years old. I remember he was arrested when a girl was shot in the eye from a pellet gun out of his window. The police traced the shots back and he was sent to juvenile jail for about six months in Trion for the crime. He did not commit the crime but did not fold and took the weight for it.

One time, we were trapped in his next door neighbor's apartment when the police were going to raid his. Before they got to his apartment, we got there and moved a safe full of guns and drugs and bulletproof vest out of his house but could not get out of the building to bring the stuff anywhere. So we knocked on the neighbor's door and she let us in and we hid there with the stuff right before the police came up and broke his door down expecting us to be there. They had no warrant so they had to actually break his locks with household tools they were borrowing from the neighbor whose house we were in. How crazy is that? When they got into his house, we heard them running around yelling freeze and shit of that nature. They realized no one was there and were amazed. They just knew they had us. They got suspicious of the neighbor and came back to her house asking who lived with her and was anyone there. She held her ground and told them no one was there with her and she lived with her daughter. As this interrogation was going on, her daughter arrived home from school. That backed the police off and they left. So I have to thank Marie for holding us down. We really owe you one for that. I could go on and on with near misses from the police and near death experiences from shootings but what I really want to say is how book smart this man is. He loved animals and could probably work for a vet. He knows his movies as well as any movie critic and he's the one you asked "who is that in the movie?" He writes poetry as well. He probably did not want that revealed but I can bet many people know it already. I really love this man and will continue to earn with him unless he chooses otherwise. Since the police like to play word games, I mean earn legally nowadays! I'm saying this to say that the streets suck plenty of talent away from the work field. Drugs kill many dreams. Many hustlers are smart and talented. He and I are getting another shot and we won't miss the next one.

Prison teaches you that you can live with the minimum. Yeah! A real self-esteem killer. See, you have to be able to see the difference with people saying you can live without luxury and saying you should live without luxury. Nowhere does it say that luxury isn't for you, but prison lets you know that if you did not attain it legally, you will be forced to live without it anyway. Understand that just because this time I am doing is a blessing in disguise for me doesn't mean it will be for anybody else. This is no place to live for any amount of years! Make no mistake about that. I've been able to focus these two years into a positive situation. Everyone will not be able to do so. It's a combination of how strong your mind is, added with the prison you land in, with the situation that prison puts you in. I have been mentally preparing myself for some length of a prison bid my whole teenage and adult life, which is a sad thing but it's a reality. Most men don't! Whether they sell drugs to people, do burglary, they still don't put their mind frame into the possibility of going to prison. Without that, your BID will not probably be considered a blessing. That's the point that I am trying to drill into everyone reading this book. Don't wait until it's too late. Don't let the glamour fool you. I am trying to wipe the ignorance from your mind before you're caught up into things you don't want to handle. A certain amount of ignorance is needed when you're living the street life. It blocks out your conscience and helps you stay as ruthless as you may very well need to be, to last in the streets. See, once you are not ignorant, you become more vulnerable to slipping up. Why? Because you know the consequences of your acts. You start to realize that possession of a gun can land you in prison for the 3 ½ years without even firing it. Who wants that? No money involved and you're gone for almost four years? You start to think differently. You realize that a kilo of heroin can land you in prison for 20 years. Once you start to think about the consequences, it hinders people from taking the correct action they need to make to survive in the streets. You are making plenty of money but are scared to carry the pistol, you increase the chances of being robbed or killed by the players of the game, who either stay ignorant to the life or understand the consequences and just don't give a fuck. They justify police shootings by saying that the police have to make a split second decision when they're in a situation. They get away with straight murder. Well, in the street life, playing the drug game hard requires you to make even quicker decisions than the police.

When someone comes to perpetrate a crime against you, they will not hesitate. You are not an authority figure to them, you are just prey. So it should not surprise the police or the community how so many young men are shot and killed that's playing the drug game closely. If the "authority figures" feel their lives are in jeopardy, which 9 out of 10 times it isn't, because criminals at any age, race, living in any neighborhood know the consequences for shooting a police officer, then how much danger does one dealer pose to another? So don't think that you can do what I was lucky enough to do and get a BID under my belt before I decided to hang up the life. Most times, it doesn't work out like that. STOP immediately and put your hustler mind to something else to earn your money. If your idea becomes a success, it most likely will bring you way more riches than the average hustler will end up making in his drug or robbery career. Even if you do well for six months a year or two years, once you add the fun and notoriety up with the money you earned, it will be usually negated out with the amount of jail time you do. It would seem to be for nothing. If you even live to see that conclusion. I lift my head and see this clown in the bed cleaning his ears. Who wants to see that early in the morning for years? Not me, not anyone. I want to gather up all of the soldiers that were in my world who played the game and played it hard and stood for the principles while they played it and start some legal business. Put OUR heads together and take a small piece of the legal pie. The guys made the illegal work so I know they can make the legal work with all the legal and positive people we have access to, we can put a major dent in an industry of our choice.

Nas said something to me one in Miami. We were down there with some people from our neighborhood. It stuck with me until today. I have always thought about what he said from time to time and wondered just what he meant by it. As all the fellows from our neighborhood were rolling around to find a restaurant and the younger guys were flirting with the girls, everyone was conversing. Nas turned to me and said, "It's crazy because if I were not a rapper, I wouldn't be here with y'all." I laughed it off, well, at least tried to, and he said, "No, I am serious. I wouldn't be here." I didn't know how to respond to that. It made me think hard about what he was trying to say. I know other people heard him but it seemed like his comment went over their heads. We moved on and ended up at a restaurant eating on Ocean Drive, where some dudes from Detroit joined us for lunch because they were fans of Nas. Jungle end up insulting them dudes about Nas not paying for the dudes meals and they pulled out plenty of money, dropped it down and walked out. Needless to say, Nas was upset with his younger brother, but Jungle did not give a fuck. After everyone went to their separate hotels, I told my cousin what Nas had said. He asked me what I thought he meant by that. I always figured it was like how I felt when I first saw the sunset in Hawaii or when I hugged Jamie Foxx by the pool in his mansion. At those instances, I felt that if I didn't sell drugs, those moments would never have happened. I guess Nas thought that if he had not become a famous rapper, he wouldn't be able to roll with the A class hustlers or goons from the neighborhood down in Miami. I wish I could have gotten confirmation of what he meant but I never did and I thought about that statement ever since. See if he was thinking that he was wrong, just like I was wrong to think I would've never made it to those two locations without drug money. I own two different timeshares, of course I could go to Hawaii on them. Nas grew up with us and was cool with everyone in the projects. The same way we ran into other, people from the neighborhood down there that didn't have money, if he wasn't rich and ran into us down there, it still would have been the same love, at least from me. I don't lean on people for shit so if I would have seen him and his brother down there and they were not popular or rich, I still would have offered to eat lunch with them and probably try and scoop some chicks. He always had the pretty girls chasing him. So did I! I kind of think I understand his point in the statement and I feel it was a real deep thought, but on my road to enlightenment, I can see that he was wrong as I was wrong with my example of Hawaii or the mansion. We had deep thoughts in shallow water. We can be anywhere, meet anyone, and accomplish anything no matter what the circumstance. Strong people make their way to get what they want. It doesn't have to be drug dealing or Hip-Hop. Hip-Hop is a good profession if it works out though. It's also legal and is also one of the few things our people created, Black and Latino.

Voting is very important in the minority community, for a number of reasons. If we don't elect our local officials, than we don't get to open the businesses our people would like to have. You have the wrong people trying to understand our needs, if they're trying to understand at all. The process of everything we want to do becomes more difficult. It's a snowball effect. Let's take New York City, if you are having a fight with someone outside of your race and call them a name in the heat of the fight, you can be charged with a hate crime. If it's a white Jewish person or homosexual, you will most likely be charged with a hate crime. Why has this law been enforced so much? Simply because these are the men and women who have the power in our city. They fight dirty, but through the law. If they don't like the way things are in the city, they vote their people in that have their interest at heart and change the law. If we as minorities did the same, we'd have a better chance of staying off the streets and out of trouble. A friend of mine opens restaurants. Very clever man. My friend (brother) comes from a great middle class income family. The McMichael's owned their own home (co-op) in L.I.C. / Astoria and sent all of the children to private school. Brian (my friend, brother) and a lot of his friends went to private school, their families also did well. Maybe that's where he got the business bug. Anyway, in Astoria, Queens, the neighborhood is very diverse. The projects have most of the poor Blacks and Latinos and even Chinese and Whites. As we grew up, most of the Chinese and Whites moved out of the projects. Other parts of the area have Greek, Italian, Spanish, Jews, etc. It's a really a good melting pot. Many businesses flourish in the area. Restaurants line the Vernon Blvd. blocks, the 30th Avenue strip, Broadway strip and Steinway Street. Brian had restaurants in a couple of those restaurant areas. One thing I noticed is that he always had to sweat and worry when it came time for him to get a liquor license. Why? He has no criminal record at all! It's because of the way things work. You have to pass the Community Board to get the OK to have a liquor license, which goes back to voting. If we had our own people in positions on the board, we wouldn't have to worry about being approved for licenses and other things when starting a business in our own neighborhoods. The Greeks and the Italians in our neighborhood have bar after bar and they get approved and they stay open even after there is an incident at their establishments. We have to be wiser and help ourselves get into positions of real power. That starts with the vote.

I hear on the radio or on TV where Republicans speak insulting our President all the time. The first, and probably the only Black President. The insults to me should be considered hate crimes. They aren't and no one gets chastised for saying them. Why? The people behind them are in power. If I call a gay a faggot at the wrong place and wrong time, I can be arrested and the charges enhanced because it's considered a hate crime, but you can make fun and insult the President of the United States on television or radio and there are no consequences. That's totally insane. I guess only the wealthy and powerful can exercise their freedom of speech, because in the ghettos, you better tread lightly. We have to vote on the smallest things to the biggest elections to make a change. In grade school, I ran for president of my school P.S 111. I won with a landslide. It was fulfilling. I was also the president of my class and the G.O. president. They were run like real elections with debates in the auditorium, etc. I was 10 or 11 years old and was being taught a valuable lesson. I wish I would have taken more heed to it. I wish I was going to realize how valuable those lessons were going to be for the rest of my life.

When I speak about this prison I am in, I refer to it as a jail heaven. What I mean by that is that with all the problems and lifestyle you have to endure here, it's probably not going to get better than this. When I arrived, the sergeant told me it was a privilege for me to land in the prison for my first bid and not to fuck it up. I thought he couldn't be serious. One, it's no privilege being in anyone's prison and two, this would be my last bid. This is just the way these police are trained to think. They assume the black man will keep them employed by coming back and forth to prison. So, when you are living in a cubicle among 50 to 60 men living out of lockers, I'm telling you that I am in jail heaven. When you are once again dependent on your mother, wife, girlfriend, or whoever so you feel less than a man, I am telling you that this is heaven. When your family takes a 16 hour bus ride to see you for 6 hours with limited contact in nasty weather, where the winters could be until June, I am telling you that I'm in heaven. Using towels to cover the stalls so you can have a little bit of privacy to use in the bath room, sharing one or two televisions to share among 50 men from different cultures, having two telephones where the gangs make sure they have ample amount of time to speak to their friends and family, which gives everyone else smaller time frames to speak to their loved ones, this is heaven in prison. Well, this isn't the way most people picture heaven I bet. It sounds more like hell. The reason I call it heaven is because the police are not as strict as in other prisons. The population of inmates isn't as large as in other prisons. The cuttings are to a minimum here. Most people catch tickets for drugs or dirty urine. Overall, the violence is to a minimum. That's why I call it jail heaven. I expected to be dropped in a ruthless spot with cuttings and stabbings every day. I mean that's the kind of guys that I ran with as a child. Most of my friends did time in rough prisons so that's what I expected. I remember Ocean and Spank, while I visited them in Comstock telling me of rats running around their cells each night. I remember Justice telling me he was with the infamous Larry Davis, and how inmates threw shit on him in his cell. This was a man that shot six cops. He also ended up being murdered in prison.

I've been told stories of correction officers that have tattoos of black babies on their hands with the baby in a noose. How fucking intimidating would that be for a person that just made it upstate and have to see that? He'll instantly think back to slavery days. He would think he could be killed in that prison not just by the inmates but by the correction officers. Yes some prisons are really hell on earth. So I'm saying this so people understand, really understand that even in the best situation that you can land in a prison term that it's a bad situation. Yes, I'm in heaven when we're comparing a bunch of bad situations, but in no way should you not understand that this could break you down mentally if not physically, as well as the people who love you. People find themselves in here sometimes and they realized that the streets are not for them. Maybe they find religion just to keep them walking straight when they get out.

Nothing is wrong with that. Hopefully, they will continue to walk with their God and not just hang on to him for the prison ride then decide they don't need Him. That would seem like you only found God out of fear. Never do or don't do something, just out of fear alone.

Fear got most men in prison in the first place. Fear of not playing by the rules the world said to play by. I was one of them. One of them that had that type of fear, but I never did something or failed to do something because of fear alone. Fear can catch up to a man that thinks he is fearless. Fear is a natural emotion. It's how you deal with it that separates men from boys in prison. Here, you can come to prison with this big reputation of making millions of dollars, and many people will honor that and will try to be in your favor. There's also a percentage of wolves that could care less about how much money you've earned in the streets. That does not make you a solid or a stand up dude. These guys will come to confront you. These men will want what you have with threats of killing you if you don't give it up. Can you deal with these type of men? This prison has inmates that probably have no one sending them packages so they are living off the land. Yeah, that baller shit is out of the window now. The respect goes to the killers and robbers on the other side of the wall, not men who can't, stomach violence. Fear sets in on these street legends for getting money and their life could forever be changed. My friend Fat Joe, God bless the dead, told me of a conversation that changed his thought pattern. He was in Federal prison for getting caught with half a kilo of cocaine which belonged to the both of us up in Harlem. He was sentenced to three years in Federal prison. He met all types of criminals from all walks of life on his brief bid. One thing stuck out to him, which he passed to me. A dude from Washington D.C. was arguing with a New York inmate about crime. The New York dude was from Harlem talking about the legends of Harlem getting money and how he was earning big money. The D.C. dude turned to him and said, "I don't care how much money you have nigga, how many bodies do you have?" Fat Joe just listened and the Harlem guy had no reply. The D.C. guy was dead serious and seemed ready to add this New York guy to his list of homicides. This is the thought pattern inside some prisons. Nobody can be fully prepared for what can happen inside, so the thing to do is stay outside. Period! Hustle for money, yes, but try the legal hustle. On a small scale, when you hear a radio advertisement or see a commercial, all that is, is a company promoting or hustling their product, but legally. You can do the same thing. We as minorities know at least one person that has access to a celebrity to some level, even if it's just that your friend has 100,000 Facebook friends. Well, promote through that forum because if there is a will, there is a way to get your thoughts to reality.

I am not a religious man to where I go to church once or twice a week. I used to go to church as a child. My uncle owned and ran a few churches and my mother made sure my sister and I went to at least a Sunday school every week. She didn't go but we had to. I believe in GOD. I believe in God because that's what I was taught to believe. I used to think of God as Jesus Christ's father and he created the world and you better be baptized and ask for forgiveness before you die or you'll go to hell. As an adult, I hang on to most of those beliefs, but now overall, I feel that there must be a high power. Call him what you want. There are just too many unexplainable things. I know this, to make a baby you need a mother, so how did the first mother get here? I dig no deeper than that. When it comes to religion, believe what you want. Religion is each individual's hope. The God I believe in, woke me up from near death experiences. Things that happened the same way to me killed other men and women. After every event that happened to me, I felt God was saying, "Kareem, you better wake up." Of course I didn't. To me, I couldn't. I had to be a good general, to lead by example, to show my crew that bullets don't stop us. We just return fire with fire. I believe that if I stopped hustling because of me almost losing my life that would be a cowardly move. I even imposed that type of thinking on other people. I certainly couldn't fold up after almost getting my leg amputated or taking a bullet to the head, stomach or back. The sick thing about it is that I would keep this life going to prove to people that I was not a coward, but the truth is I was not man enough to walk away from the life in fear of what the streets would think. Do you understand how we begin to think once in the life? I was more scared of being criticized in the streets by men and women who will probably never leave the project they grew up in, than scared of getting killed or put in prison for life. Whew! Let's move on.

When God woke me from the coma after a month, it seemed like a miracle to my family and friends. After I woke up, I still wouldn't be healthy enough to leave the hospital for six months. My body just wouldn't heal and the doctors honestly didn't know what to do. They were great doctors but it was a rare gunshot wound, so I was like an experiment, the guinea pig. After the coma, I had a bad memory. My muscles wouldn't work for not moving for so long. I hallucinated about things. I couldn't speak but thought I was yelling. I had bad pneumonia. The doctors discussed booking me in the mental ward if I didn't start responding to regular medication. When in the coma for that month, I had a nonstop dream. Imagine dreaming for a month straight. When I woke up, I thought that everything in my dream had really happened. In my dream, there were murderers and police chases and I thought that the police were going to arrest me from my hospital bed. I even told my family to bust me out of the hospital. Ha-ha! It's a little funny now, but it was no laughing matter at all. Everyone was worried sick about me. I believe I had several surgeries in one day at one point. Okay, where I am going with this, is that in that coma sleep, I also went to heaven. I saw angels and I saw a pearly gate. The fog, the white gowns, people that I know that died, the whole shabang! I tell people this and this is just one they cannot believe. It's true though, and I was told that I wasn't ready to come in yet and turned away. It seemed so real, as real as anything has ever felt to me. I believe God was once again giving me a sign. I believe he gave me so many signs and chances that it must be for something big. I must have been left alive for something big. Maybe it is to get this word out to the masses of children and teenagers that need to hear this to prevent them from making big mistakes. I am not your parent, teacher or pastor. I am a street dude with a resume to prove it. I'm talking about and warning about the route that I went down. I'm qualified to give this advice out to people. This whole book is being written from prison so there's nothing fraudulent about who is telling you to hustle legally, to educate yourself, formally as well as streetwise. I believe that this time around, this is my last shot. I had a few shots already, but this one I better make it or I will probably pay permanently. Either by death or prison. Remember most people only get one shot. Don't waste yours.

So what am I going to do, when I get back in society? Going to play the game? Yup! Play the game but legally. I really work hard, and start a business. The first business, I thought long and hard about it. I always had a sense of community in mind when I think of anything I do. I know what the people of the "lower class" want and need. I know what they qualify for and what they don't. I know because I grew up there. I partied there, I earned money there. It's my roots. The system is designed to keep everyone at the financial level that they were born into, unless they do something out of the ordinary. We have to break that cycle. Everyone needs to help. What I decided to do was to pool money from family and friends and start a company. WOODSLENDERS. It's a money lending company that's under a parent company. The purpose of this company is to lend money to small businesses which do not qualify to get the money from banks. Small loans for small startup businesses. Money can be ordered for inventory for your business that's a little behind, or small renovations or whatever is worked out legally!! This will get people to get their business plans together and know they have someone that will at least try and help them get their hair salon some new dryers or their restaurant some new tables or computers or bodega a new sign. The company can help empower certain neighborhoods. That's the step, well, the first step of putting money where my mouth is. If the kids want to start young, start a lemonade stand at the neighborhood basketball tournaments. You have to try and teach the kids that there's nothing wrong with earning a legit dollar. Show them how money works for them. Teach them to be business savvy. If we don't, someone else will, probably someone that does what I did for 25 years.

"You'll be dead or in jail." I don't remember the first time I heard that statement. I cannot remember if it was my mother who said it, or my father or just someone on the streets. The exact quote was, "If you run the streets and sell drugs, you'll either end up dead or in jail!" Oh! How I always thought that was just a saying that 'old' people told guys in the hood. The only thing was that along my street journey, I started to see my friends either getting killed or going to prison. I still didn't think that this applied to me. I was one step ahead of most guys in the street I thought. I paid closer attention to what was going on around me. I was just plain out smarter.

As I'm showering in this nasty bathroom, in the scalding hot water, I giggle sometimes as I think about how I became the second part of the statement. On four occasions, I almost ended up on the front end of that statement. Luckily, I only ended up in prison, so I can get another shot at life. Dead or in jail. I think about that a lot. Could I have beaten that statement altogether? Could I have stopped in the middle of the game, gotten a job or started a business and prove that statement wrong? I guess everyone thinks that they could. When is it right to stop? How much money is enough money? Sadly, selling drugs, you most likely will end up dead or in prison. I dwell on it and that's one of the most proven statements I've ever heard in my life. Not saying that in between that time you cannot have the time of your life. You can do things beyond your wildest dreams in between that time of death or prison. Everyone has to die one day, anyway. Death is the grand finale. Nobody wants it though. Now prison is death on earth. You are alive mentally and physically but your life having any meaning comes to a halt. You feel helpless, you are dependent on others, you are reduced from the independent person you once were. Nobody wants to feel those feelings or emotions. I struggle every day with feeling helpless to myself and to the people I love. These are the times I wish I was ignorant to many things in life so I wouldn't know what I am missing in the free world. Some people would say the real world, but let me assure you that the world of prison is very much real. In the five cubicles next to mine, they're different generations of men living in them. Next to me at 50 bed is Will, who is 54 years old, 49 bed is me at 42 years, 48 bed is Pistol at 22 years, 47 bed is Julio at 26, 46 is "L" at 38. Different generations and from different walks of life. A good friend of mine named Bernal is in that 37 bed. He's 65 years old doing five years for making a mistake that he couldn't take back. Pistol told me that his worst fear is to be back in this place at that age. This is no place to spend your Glory years. He's a good guy, we have to make sure that he gets a spot on the phone some nights when people are trying to thug out the phone line. If no one stands up for him, his wife wouldn't get a call from him some nights. I constantly stay on my toes and stay aggressive to make sure no one dares get in my way for the phone. Who the hell wants to do that every fucking day? On top of that, I am 42 years old. Once here though, you cannot make excuses or look for sympathy. At the end of the day here I am just another statistic. Staying in my cubicle, waiting for the day I can get out of this place.

I thought I could beat the odds, just like a fool walking into a casino thinking that he will leave rich from playing craps or roulette. The thing is it's in people's nature, their makeup, they are designed to still try things even knowing the odds are greatly against them. Everyone thinks that they might be the lucky one. I did. I thought that I could beat the odds if I did certain things to protect myself from death or prison, things like carrying a weapon and wearing a bullet proof vest and instilling enough fear in people where they wouldn't want any problems with me, just enough for them to be scared to want to kill me. I really thought hard about those choices. Well, I am still alive, but was put at death's doorstep several times. I also thought I made my odds better at avoiding prison by stepping away from the fiends. The users will usually be the ones who break and tell the police what they want to know after an arrest. I then even separated myself from the small dealers that I also thought may break if their backs were against the wall. You figure that they get arrested and their bail is more than the amount of money that they buy drugs with. In some cases, their bail is more money than they ever had their hands on. So at that point, they don't see the worth of hustling. You see, if they don't see the worth, they quickly want out of their predicament and look to tell. Many of my friends and even I have been arrested because of one of these types of cowards. I got as far away from an operation as one could get, while still being on top of the business. I felt the only way for me to be arrested was to actually be caught buying the kilos or getting pulled over bringing the drugs to the stash house, which the cars had secret traps so random searches by the police would also have turned up nothing. Yes, and increasing my odds, in addition to my experience, I thought I was just waiting for the right moment to stop, just like in a typical gambler. They never think the right time is now. I didn't either and I crapped out. So when is the right time? That answer is immediately. There is no hustler's manual that tells you the amount of money you should have to retire, so don't look for that certain number. Stop now!

Now let me be very clear to everyone reading this. Being legit isn't an easy thing. It's not easy for many reasons. Some reasons are not reasons of our choice. We've never had an equal playing field. Wealth in this country was not supposed to be had by our people. So in all reality, we never had a fair chance. Yes we make bad decisions to set us back further but understand that when the game started, the white man was spotted a hundred points. Our ancestors owned no wealth in this country that comes from when this country was young. Why? We were slaves when the banks started, when railroads started, when land was being sold and so on. They weren't allowed to own anything. Whichever way we turned, there was an obstacle. You may say that times have changed and we have a Black President which is true, but we cannot catch up to people's wealth when we had no input on what factors would determine what would be important in life. Okay we cannot dwell on that forever but we must understand it and explain it to our children. We must let them understand that everything will be a little bit harder for them. Less than 60 years ago, we got our civil rights. That's not long at all in terms of how old this country is. I am just mentioning this because black people have parents and grandparents that didn't get a fair shot in life. They pass that anger and animosity down to others in their family and everyone believes that we've never had a fair share and will never have one. These are not made up feelings or opinions. These are facts as our great grandparents knew it. Hostility pours back into the community and into the schools. Our people start having a sense of self-doubt. We believe in our brains that we are second class citizens and the ones that make it are lucky. These thoughts lead us to crime where we feel we can be our own bosses and excel. I don't use the nasty history of this country as an excuse for anyone but I know it could and does play an important part in why some people make the decisions they make. So when we succeed it's in spite of the history of our own country. What little freedoms they dangle in front of us we must work extra hard to use it to our advantage. Is it fair? No. But who said life was fair? We have to move fast and make the best out of the liberties we have because if too many of us are too strong, they will try and take those liberties back, by making laws against what we're doing.

So, sometimes it seems like our people are forced into crimes feeling like it's the only way to get the American dream. It might not be the right thing to do under the White man's laws but you have to at least understand where we are coming from. Let history be in the twilight zone and the White race awakens to a world where the Black man held the cards and snatched the Whites to a new land as slaves. Let the Black race be the first 42 Presidents to run the country. Let us be the people who decided from day one what's important in life. Things that we already have. Things that we control. Let us be the crew of six men that got together and found a way to legalize printing our own money (Federal Reserve)! Give us those head starts and see how great our people will be. As we Black minorities grow, in knowledge and in talent, we need to make a difference in our country.

So they sent me to Ogdensburg state prison. Really far and really cold in upstate New York. It's a small jail with less than 400 inmates living there at times, senior officers and kind of laid back. I expected to go to a different type of jail that was more rowdy, but I am cool with this type of the prison life because it gives me the time to study and build my mind right. With the CMC status, I know that it's one of the reasons they sent me to this small jail. In case I tried to start some type of drug business in here, it would be easily detected. Someone would probably snitch or the police would just find out because of how small this place is. That never was on my agenda, anyway. The place is also bad for your family visiting. The snow stays on the ground until June sometimes. My family prefers to drive instead of the bus but I wouldn't want them to and fuck with the elements of Mother Nature. I decided that they should take the bus which forces them to see me less or they could fly, which is way more expensive. Bottom line is that a person with less finances and less of a good relationship with their family and friends can really just forget about visits up here. These things should be in a person's thought process as they are planning the next robbery or burglary or murder. Remember the game is 360°and the more you deal in reality, the more prepared you are for the consequences and maybe you will decide that the person doesn't deserve to be robbed or murdered when you weigh the crime against the punishment. I'm saying that some things aren't worth doing, period. I land in a jail with my main damn man, truly lil brother that I helped groom to be the pure player in the game that he was. Nas even shouted him out on his last album. I take a little credit for that because Manolo has lived in QB his whole life and was hustling for at least half of it and Nas has been writing albums since the early nineties and he never mentioned the young hustler before. After I got to him he started to put real tangible shit on the streets and brought things of real value and started not just going to the state where events like All- star weekend was or Floyd Mayweather was fighting, he started to attend these events. Even sitting ringside at prize fights. He went from pants hanging off his ass to his pants being tailored. One of the best from QB as far as hustling is concerned. He had the toys to prove it. Check the indictment. Biggie said, "Niggas talking it but aint living it," but he was. His run stopped short because of my indictment that spread to a wire on his phone (which was probably illegal). He ended up taking a flat five years for weapons and drug charges which started out as A-1 felony. We end up in the same spot in the same housing area about 10 cubes apart. Wow, really weird. The hood thinks it's not by accident and that the police are still on us. The hood wants to believe those farfetched stories but hey, I thought an investigation on me with wired phones and video surveillance was farfetched as well. He isn't sitting around doing nothing. He's attacking his conviction every chance he gets. See we don't care if you caught us playing the game but we damn sure will not let you cheat at doing it.

He sees plenty of constitutional laws that were stepped on to put us behind bars, which explains the sentences we received for committing what they consider to be the worst drug crimes you can do. I had major drug trafficking and director of criminal organization, along with a gun charge and possession of drugs and last but not least, conspiracy. These charges hold a life sentence. He got caught with over half a kilo of cocaine, two pounds of weed, four guns, two were assault weapons and a suppressor, and 20k in cash and he received five years. So either they were the nicest District Attorneys in the business or there is an air of wrongdoing on the police part. Manolo is trying to get to the bottom of this and hopefully he does. Any other free time he has though is used reading up on the Tech industry and thinking of plenty of problems in the world that an invention of his can make right. His view of getting to the top is a little different from mine but we're both focused on getting there. I see prison different from him. I accept this sentence. I turn the negative to positive. He, on the other hand, wants out! He has no problem telling me that every day. I mean he's chilling out and has everything that a nigga could want and need in prison, but I guess he doesn't come to accept this nasty way of life as the norm and he wants out, every day!! LOL, shit is real funny sometimes. We keep each other strong and focused while we do this B.I.D. As I am writing this, I look up and down at his cube and he's mopping his floor. I smile because if anyone knows Manolo, you would think that he keeps his cube germ free and he really tries to. I have a bunch of pictures on my wall of people from all different years of my life. A wall full of growth and change. It makes me see I was a semi-criminal mastermind. Nah but it shows I had a good life. That part of my life is over though.

I hope in a few years, I'll have new pictures with the same people looking just as happy because my new endeavors in life went as well or better than my old ones. This time, looking at the pictures from one of my homes that I have acquired legally. I lay in my cube, look at pictures and think of stories of things I've done with some of the people in the flicks. I have one with Dash, Skins and me at Wendy Williams Don's and Diva's party she used to throw in Manhattan or Jersey every year. We all had gators sneakers on and Coogi sweaters and I had on the brown mink. Skins was so educated but just couldn't shake that street life even after going to college all the way in West V.A, got his BA there but also three year Federal bid for drugs. I remember he used to have a cop friend of ours driving to the south with drugs. I don't even think he told her but knew if stopped, they'd probably be safe because she was a cop and he was a college student. Shit I am pretty sure she didn't know because she was real scary to be a NYPD cop. I remember sitting in my truck one day with Raymond and a few others and this cop and her friends pulled up on us to see what we were up to. She was off duty so she was in plain clothes. The detectives pulled up and started questioning us. We had a bottle of champagne or Hennessey in the car and thought these dudes would give us a hard time. So her being a cop and all, I thought she would pull her badge or identify herself as a cop and they would leave. No way! She got nervous fearing one of us had a gun on us. She made sure that the detectives knew her and her friends had just arrived and wasn't aware of anything we had. Everything turned out OK but damn! With cop friends like that who needs enemies, for crying out loud! Nah I guess that's the reputation we built that she just couldn't take that risk. She and I are still good friends till this day.

So what was all this writing about? Yes it was to tell the true story about a teenager turned man in the drug game and the journey it took me on. It also was to inform young men and women all around the country that the life of hustling drugs has two sides: the side with glitz and glamour, which I lived, even though in my eyes it wasn't lived on an extraordinary level, but on the level I played most drug dealers will never see that level. That's just a true fact. The other side of the game that I also saw the violence, addictions, betrayal, sadness and prison. Most hustlers will see that side of the game. Most won't be so lucky to get charged with an A-1 felony of major trafficking and be able to fight it and get a two-year sentence. That's highly unlikely. Most people will get the lengthy prison sentences with little to nothing to show for it. They most likely will be in prison talking about money they never actually had, hoping that their girlfriend, wife, whoever will visit or send them a package. I know a few high ranking Bloods that are in NYS prisons. A few are very close to me. One who I won't name but is as tough as nails is heading toward the 20-year mark in prison in about five years. A friend of ours visits him as well as me. He told her that he wished that he could take it all back. He's locked up for a quadruple shooting where two people were killed and the police ended up shooting him as well. He and I used to drive around in my Lexus and cruise the neighborhood feeling like hood Kings. He was younger than me by five years so he was very young in 1994 when I bought my first Lexus. We were both young. See, he doesn't have a chance to do this life over, but he now wishes he did. Not saying that he's getting weak on the inside but a motherfucker wants freedom, a life with a family of his own. So out of respect for him and all my other friends with life sentences that won't get another chance, I must get on the path of legality. What, should I keep pushing the envelope until I share a cell with one of them? I think not. It's time for all the youngsters from the inner city to refocus their brainpower to make legal businesses, to finish formal schooling and take that education along with their street sense and start businesses. Invest in their communities. To vote, to get people who look like us into office to be able to help change the neighborhoods. We need to not just vote at the presidential elections, but at the local and city elections, where the officials affect us more personally. The president governs the country. We need to look for people that govern us more personally. Every election counts, not just when P. Diddy says it or Jay-Z, who by the way are part of the one percent that own over 90% of the wealth of this country. Use Jay-Z, 50 Cent, Dr. Dre, President Barack Obama, Oprah Winfrey and the numerous other successful blacks as people to look at and say, "I can do it too."

See, I didn't make the most money. That's not what makes me unique; it's my longevity that makes me unique. My preparation for the consequences makes me unique. So ask yourself before you step into the drug game, what makes you unique? What makes you think you can stay one step ahead of the police and the killers? Can you fix your mind to cope with being put in a wheelchair for a period of time, or maybe for life? Can you adjust to life in prison? Do you know your limits? Or will you fold like a weak man? Will you let the state or government persuade you that taking someone else's life apart is the best thing for you to do? I mean why play with fire? Why bite off more than you can swallow? More than you want to swallow? Let me put it like this: if you're prepared to take a bullet to the head, then one in the toe and three in the leg and one in the stomach on two different incidents, then add one more to the head and two by your hip, then top it off with one to your back on the last occasion, then welcome to the game. If you're prepared to be put in a wheelchair for six months with the threat of getting your leg amputated, hey then welcome the game. If you won't panic when guns are put to your head and you are laid down on your face with two close friends in a project apartment while being robbed, then by all means live that life. Don't forget about the sleeping around 50 men every night for years, the going back and forth to court shackled, waiting to receive a sentence. The gangsters cutting people maybe even you, then join the life of a hustler. These are the things I had to endure during my run in the streets hustling. Those things, all of them, happened to me! Things are worse for some people. I believed that those types of atrocities were normal for young men in the inner city, but they weren't. These things should not happen but they became normal to us. We see our fathers, uncles, sisters and aunts commit acts of violence all over drugs and this violence just simply becomes our way of life. It will take more than just one book to get the inner-city to change but as the saying goes, Each One Teach One.

So yes, I bought over 35 cars since I was 17, bought hundreds of thousands of dollars' worth of jewelry and watches, travelled the world, did big boxing events from when Mike Tyson was Iron Mike to when Floyd Mayweather Jr. was the biggest draw. Anyone that played the game knows that was from the nineties to the next century! Met plenty of stars, did shows from the Apollo, Radio City and the Beacon theatre with different rappers over the years without having one song, I still graced the stage. Award shows from the infamous Source Awards where the East Coast/West Coast beef really ignited to the 2013 BET Awards. Longevity is what I was mostly respected for. Longevity while playing by the gangster rules, the code of the streets. Was it worth it? For me, I have no regrets but I would not recommend it. The odds of being a true drug dealer superstar are worse than the odds of being a professional athlete. Or the odds of becoming a multimillionaire rapper-very slim. I suggest that you take that entrepreneurial spirit, with the street education along with the formal education and set some goals and go after them. Dream big, then think big then capture your dream. Love yourself. Also love your family who suffers every time you are arrested. They suffer every time you're shot at or stabbed. Be a boss for real. Be a real general and lead men to success legally. I didn't tell my story from one side; I told it how it was. As I said before, there's plenty of other violent, rough, and unimaginable things that happened in my life that were not mentioned. I could start over and tell a different episode of my street life encounters, but I think you got the point already. I started writing this book from the boat jail in the Bronx. I am ending it off from Dorm E2, Cube 49 up in Ogdensburg Correctional Facility.

EPILOGUE

This book that I poured my heart into is my attempt to take the experiences from bad events and use them as illustrations to get people to get some good out of them. Meaning these wicked and painful experiences should open the eyes of everyone whose eyes have been closed to the harsh way of life that I as well as thousands of poor children have to see or experience. I use these bad situations to let people know the cost of playing the drug game. I use these situations to show the powers that be that from crime many people think it's the only way to accomplish the American dream. The Kennedy family used crime to prosper and is one of the most loved families in history. They changed their criminal behavior around and made it to the top of the government totem pole. This country allows people that opportunity to change. So don't take my truths out of context and think I am just grandstanding or bragging about my criminal life, because if I wasn't through with it I wouldn't be talking about it. Sorry if I cannot take a firmer stance about certain issues but I am just a realist. The black and Latino struggle will continue. Police will keep killing us, having felonies will keep us stagnated. Some states are even trying to make it harder to keep our voting rights for people without felonies. So crime will stay part of

America. It will stay part of the poor communities unless more opportunities become available and things become fairer.

Made in the USA
Middletown, DE
17 May 2021